THE COMMONWEALTH AND INTERNATIONAL LIBRARY
Joint Chairmen of the Honorary Editorial Advisory Board
SIR ROBERT ROBINSON, O.M., F.R.S., LONDON
DEAN ATHELSTAN SPILHAUS, MINNESOTA
Publisher: ROBERT MAXWELL, M.C., M.P.

Advances in the Teaching of Modern Languages

Advances in the Teaching of Modern Languages

VOLUME TWO

Edited by

G. MATHIEU

PERGAMON PRESS
OXFORD · LONDON · EDINBURGH · NEW YORK
TORONTO · SYDNEY · PARIS · BRAUNSCHWEIG

Pergamon Press Ltd., Headington Hill Hall, Oxford
4 & 5 Fitzroy Square, London W.1

Pergamon Press (Scotland) Ltd., 2 & 3 Teviot Place, Edinburgh 1

Pergamon Press Inc., 44-01 21st Street, Long Island City, New York 11101

Pergamon of Canada, Ltd., 6 Adelaide Street East, Toronto, Ontario

Pergamon Press (Aust.) Pty. Ltd., 20-22 Margaret Street, Sydney,
New South Wales

Pergamon Press S.A.R.L., 24 rue des Écoles, Paris 5ᵉ

Vieweg & Sohn GmbH, Burgplatz 1, Braunschweig

Copyright © 1966 Pergamon Press Inc.
First edition 1966
Library of Congress Catalog Card No. 64-9271

Printed in Great Britain by The Whitefriars Press Ltd.

This book is sold subject to the condition
that it shall not, by way of trade, be lent,
resold, hired out, or otherwise disposed
of without the publisher's consent,
in any form of binding or cover
other than that in which
it is published.

(2810/66)

Contents

	INTRODUCTION	vii
I.	Oklahoma Revisited *by Pierre Delattre*	1
II.	A Model for Research in Programmed Self-instruction *by John B. Carroll*	11
III.	A Study of Programmed Self-instruction for Seventh-grade Learners *by Gerald Newmark*	47
IV.	Toward Self-instruction in Foreign Language Learning *by Albert Valdman*	76
V.	Programming Second Language Reading *by George A. C. Scherer*	108
VI.	The Pauseless Tape in Programmed Pattern Drills *by G. Mathieu*	130
VII.	Modern Greek Self-taught: First Step to a National Library *by Paul Pimsleur*	138
VIII.	Closing the Circle: Training the Teachers' Teachers *by Jack M. Stein*	147
IX.	Observation of Demonstration Classes as a Method of Teaching Teachers *by F. W. Nachtmann*	164
X.	A Model Design for the In-service Training of Foreign Language Teachers *by David M. Feldman*	173
XI.	Continuum in Language Learning *by Everett V. O'Rourke*	183
XII.	Prospects for FLES *by Roger A. Pillet*	196
	ABOUT THE CONTRIBUTORS	211

Introduction

THE revolution in foreign language teaching that is currently sweeping away traditional methods and approaches was surveyed by B. Libbish, editor of Volume One of this series (1964), in his Introduction. He concluded: "There is still much to be done. We are merely on the fringe of the new procedures." Volume Two, which offers twelve articles by pioneers in modern language teaching, is an attempt to show some of the steps that have been taken in the development of new procedures. Yet we can but echo: "There is still much to be done."

Advances in any field can be effectively accomplished only if information about new developments are made as widely and rapidly available as possible. One of the main purposes of this series is to do just that: to make contributions quickly and easily accessible to teachers and researchers, wherever they may be. The modern language profession—and this includes English as a foreign or second language—has been until recently notoriously remiss in disseminating information about its "advances". In other fields, the teaching profession is far more alert to current research. For instance, it would be unthinkable for a physics teacher to go merrily on teaching that molecule XYZ spins from left to right when more than a year earlier an article in *The Ruritanian Journal of Physics* reported that it spins from right to left. Yet, to give an example from the English area of our own field, thousands of teachers go merrily on asserting that most nouns in English form their plurals by "adding an *s* or *es*", whereas linguists long ago told us that plurals are formed by adding either an unvoiced sibilant [s] as in *lamps,* or a voiced sibilant [z] as in *bees,* preceded under certain conditions by [ə].

The lack of communication among teachers of the same language is serious enough, but in our field it is compounded by the almost desperate absence of communication among teachers of different languages or of related disciplines outside of our specialization.

How many teachers of French read *The German Quarterly*? How many teachers of German have ever glanced at *Hispania*? And how many professors of any language have ever deigned believe that *Audiovisual Instruction, The International Review of Education*, the *Journal of Speech and Hearing Science* or the *Psychological Review* might contain an article which has direct bearing on what they should or should not do every day in class? The profession can only "advance" if it keeps itself informed on all fronts, and today language teaching has many more fronts than a decade ago. The battles are fought on the fronts of acoustics and neurology, of electronics and school management, to mention but a few.

It is impossible in any compendium to report developments on all fronts, and the present volume covers just two: Man and Machine. Automation looms large before us. Professor Delattre's twenty-year retrospect—with which we open our anthology—clearly points the way to the need for collaboration between Man and Machine. Today it is evident from many controlled experiments that machine-taught students in beginning foreign language courses are as good as, if not better than, the man-taught ones. The teaching of foreign languages, with the need for habit-forming exercises such as drills and memorization, is natural material for the machine. Hence six contributions deal specifically with advances on the front of programmed learning and man's exploitation of the machine as a presentation device. However, it will be many, many years before the machine can hope to displace the human teacher, if indeed it ever can. Meanwhile, we need teachers—teachers who are at least as good as the machine. Three contributions address themselves to the crucial problem of the professional preparation of future teachers and the continuing "re-training" of teachers now in service.

But Man and Machine is not quite enough. There is also the Administrator. One of the happy innovations brought about by the language revolution is the ever-increasing dialogue between the foreign language teacher and the administrator. And frequently, as in the case of Mr. Everett V. O'Rourke, the foreign language profession receives its best support on the administrative front from school management experts who have never taught a foreign language.

Lastly, no report on advances in foreign languages can ignore the most important front: the elementary school. According to Professor Pillet the success of FLES promises to make significant changes in our approaches to second language teaching and learning. And we join him in his optimism, for the choice may well be FLES (Foreign Languages in the Elementary Schools) or FLOP (Foreign Languages for Older People).

Fullerton, California G. MATHIEU

CHAPTER I

Oklahoma Revisited

PIERRE DELATTRE
University of California, Santa Barbara

A LITTLE over twenty years ago, the University of Oklahoma Modern Language Department gave us the opportunity to make an experiment in language teaching which influenced our whole career and for which we shall always be grateful. After twenty years of continuous experience with audio-lingual techniques, we would like to re-examine objectively this experiment and the teaching precepts that were drawn from it at the time.

Many of us can remember that, just before the war, language teaching methods had reached an all-time low. Modern languages were mostly being taught as dead languages. The baleful influence of Latin grammar combined with teachers' apathy, produced, after three or four years of language study, a student who could read for translation, perhaps even write the language, but who could not understand it aurally, much less speak it. The first news of this deplorable condition reached the press and the government when young soldiers, assigned because of their college record to posts that required some knowledge of a foreign language, proved themselves incapable of communicating orally with the natives of the foreign country where they were stationed. Officers who had counted on their educated men became indignant and urgently requested a reform of the teaching methods in the United States.

The example of effective language teaching was set by the armed forces themselves. They organized a program based on audio-lingual methods, with the help of acetate disc recordings at 78 revolutions per minute. (Neither the long-playing records at 33 rpm nor the magnetic tapes had yet been developed.) The use of "informants" in the classroom was initiated—native speakers of the target language would be assigned to each class to take charge of all oral drills, leaving to the regular instructor only the discussions on grammatical structure. This was not very flattering to the competence of the instructor, but more important than the respect due to a professor was the matter of winning a war.

Colleges and universities, humiliated by the criticism and stimulated by the Army experiments, soon organized experiments of their own to study the possibility of teaching languages by purely audio-lingual methods. In one of these experiments, performed at the University of Oklahoma, the advantages of the oral method over the traditional one became most apparent. The same instructor taught two first-year courses in French concurrently. In one of them he used the same textbook as the previous year from the first day, allowing the students to see the written form of the words they were learning to pronounce, and to study grammar rules before doing composition and translation exercises in writing. In this manner, reading and writing naturally had to precede aural understanding and speaking. In the other class, the French instructor used no book whatsoever, and allowed no writing during the whole first semester.

In the experimental class, the students learned first from the voice of the teacher in class, then finished learning ("overlearning") from a record after class. Each day a new record was cut, the length of which was gauged to the amount of audio material the students had been able to absorb the previous day. Instead of learning grammar—that is, correctness of expression according to tradition— by rules and written exercises, they learned it by addition, substitution, and transformation drills which they could hear from the record of the day but could never see. This forced them to make oral responses to aural stimuli. Instead of learning passively and partially, knowing that they could refer back to a book at any time, the students of the experimental audio-lingual class had to learn actively and completely whatever they heard before going on to something new. Forming the habit of relying exclusively on aural stimuli was a struggle for them; the impulse to put down in writing the material that came from the loudspeaker was violent at first and required strict control on the part of the instructor, but this resistance to the purely aural lasted less than a week. As soon as a few utterances, questions and answers had become orally automatic to the student, the audio-lingual aspect of learning was accepted and great satisfaction was experienced.

In the experimental class, digesting new material had to be complete and required considerable repetition and constant review; therefore the quantity that could be added each day was extremely small as compared with the amount that was being learned passively by the class using the traditional method. It soon became apparent that, as long as the teaching was entirely audio-lingual, quantity would have to be replaced by quality, and that the daily gain in vocabulary would be very limited.

In order to help students acquire a near native pronunciation from the start, the phonetic difficulties of the first three weeks of material were carefully graded. The material of the first week included only the vowels [i], [ɛ], [ə], and [a], with no R consonant and no semivowel [ɥ], thus reducing the articulatory difficulty to a minimum. But it was during this first week, with the most simple segmental phonemes, that the suprasegmental (or prosodic) features were taught: correct habits of intonation, rhythm, stress, and syllabication were acquired before the complete sound system was introduced. This made it possible to practice and improve the prosodic features while learning new sounds during the second and third weeks. The second week introduced all the rounded vowels, the consonant R and the semivowel [j]. And the third week completed the phonemic structure with nasal vowels and the semivowel [ɥ]. From then on, the learning sequences concentrated on grammatical structures of morphology and syntax rather than on vocabulary. The acquisition of vocabulary was left for the very last stage, in the second semester, when reading out of a book was permitted.

Parallel testing of the two classes took place at regular intervals. By the end of the first semester, the vocabulary of the experimental class was much smaller than that of the traditional class. Nevertheless, the audio-lingual students could understand and express themselves better at French table (open to all) than the book students. By the end of the year, the audio-lingual students had caught up with the others in vocabulary and were far superior to them in understanding and in speaking. They were also slightly superior to the book students in grammar—they made fewer grammatical mistakes in composition exercises.

This experiment was repeated several years later at the University of Texas, on a larger scale (several classes in each controlled group), using exactly the same material, and the results were quite similar. The audio-lingual students were not only superior in aural understanding and in oral expression, but they also received slightly higher grades in written composition exercises at the end of the year.

The Problem of Right Spelling

The weakness of the audio-visual students was in spelling. Apparently, their memory of words was related only to *sound images* and the difficulty they had in establishing a logical relation between the French sounds and the *graphic images* that characterize them presented an obstacle to retention. Just as, during the first week of instruction, the audio-lingual students resisted giving up the writing habit, so, at the beginning of the second semester, they were upset upon discovering how French was spelled, and they could not readily adjust to the graphic form.

Is spelling worthy of respect in any case? It does not appear to be if we consider that it is our own generation that has made of correct spelling the sort of shibboleth it is today. Knowing the dictionary spelling used to be the concern of working men, the typesetters. Voltaire and other writers of his age could not spell (that is, they could not spell according to the dictionary), or perhaps they did not care to. Voltaire wrote the same word three different ways on the same page, but he could think: what he said could stand the test of time. Today, many are those who confuse being educated with being able to spell according to the dictionary, because of the misleading emphasis that was placed on this futility during their early school years.

Linguists have made us realize that the written word is not the word itself nor even the concept it communicates but merely a graphic form that symbolizes the natural form of the word—the sound form which is produced by a mouth, heard by an ear, and perceived by a brain, thanks to learned habits. It is the recognition of such facts that led George Bernard Shaw to donate his personal fortune for a reform of English spelling. Many other great men of letters have similarly perceived the necessity of a reform.

"In French, to write well one must write as one does not pronounce", said Paul Valery. Marcel Clédat, in his speech of acceptance of membership in the French Academy, called the dictionary "the list of compulsory mistakes of spelling" on the ground that, of the etymologies reflected by orthography, very few were correct or rationally applied (*il fasse* should be written *il face*, like *il lace; eu* should be written *û*, like *dû, poids* should be *pois,* like *mois,* and so on, ad infinitum). Vendryes, the late dean of the University of Paris, knew who was to blame for this state of things: "Our language has suffered more than any other from the bad influence of pedantic scholars who created all those complications and errors of orthography in the sixteenth century." (*Le Langage*, p. 395.) And more recently, Raymond Queneau, the humoristic author of *Zazie,* but also the serious editor of the Pléiade Collection, writes in *Batons, Chiffres et Lettres*:

> When one is aware of the malleable nature of the sentence and the word, he cannot admit the everlasting tyranny of modern spelling ... A spelling reform, or rather the adoption of a phonetic orthography, is imperative; it will demonstrate what is essential: the pre-eminence of the oral over the written ... Spelling is worse than a bad habit, it is a vanity." [pp. 20–21.]

Furthermore, it is not on spelling that one bases one's esthetic appreciation of a language. The printed line is but a mask. Once this mask is lifted and the sound alone is perceived, not only does the true linguistic structure of a language appear, but its esthetic qualities can be sensed as well. French, which is so handicapped by its faulty spelling, regains its natural dignity, its original qualities of clarity and sonority, when direct contact with the speech sounds can be made. Then it reveals a rich and varied system of vowels and consonants in which frontal resonance predominates, open syllables that are proud of their vowels, oxytonic accentuation that emphasizes the last syllables of sense groups not by heavy marks of intensity but by restrained increases of length, an intonation capable of contrasting the lightest shades of syntactic meaning, a rhythm of equal syllables which recalls a string of pearls. The most characteristic sounds of French are perhaps the nasal vowels, often described by poets as diffuse and mellow, but seldom appreciated as much as they are in these touching lines written by a Japanese friend of ours with a rare capacity for listening to the sounds alone:

> While there are no languages which do not contain nasal sounds in their phone-system, there are only a few having nasal sounds in their vowel group. One of these is French. The French nasalized-vowel quality seems to us to be unrivaled for attractiveness. The characteristic nuance of French speech is owing in part to its rich nasal quality. One is attracted by its charm, especially when misty nasals are uttered by a glossy voice, for example, in an alto tone of moderate pitch. In French conversation, and particularly in the prosodical reading of French verse, nasalized vowels appear in sweet relief in the sequential stream of speech waves. This mode of beauty seems to suggest that nasally-modulated vowels are brought into exquisite contrast with oral vowels, thereby giving forth some spell by the pleasing rhythmical alternation of timbres between orals and nasals, thus presenting alternating bright gay lustrous and shadowy gloomy nebulous timbres. This suggestion leads us to the very problem of distinction between orality and nasality in their essential meaning. Figuratively speaking, the timbre pattern of orality focusses images on the sunny side and that of nasality conversely focusses images on the shadowy side.

Such sensitive judgments can only be made after listening to the sound of a language, not after looking at its graphic form. The aural-oral aspect of a language is not limited to audio-lingual teaching; it also concerns the esthetic appreciation of its sounds.

Principles Derived from Oklahoma Experiment

But let us return to the Oklahoma experiment and see what lesson can be derived from it. The results of this experiment seem to show that, in the teaching of a foreign language as a living language, three kinds of habits must be acquired before making use of a book.

1. Most important of all are the purely *psychological* habits, which consist in relating sound to meaning without the interference of graphic symbols. During the initial stage of language learning the sound of a word and its concept must be directly connected. Probably the graphic symbols of languages such as German, Spanish, Italian, Russian, Finnish, which are nearly phonetic, are less harmful than those of French or English. But we believe that all visual images are detrimental to the formation of aural-oral habits, even those of phonetic symbols. If phonetic notation is useful, it is later, perhaps at a third stage, well after the rules of spelling have been mastered. Direct association of sound and meaning is the only road to success in language teaching, and the most difficult problem is to provoke this direct association by appropriate techniques and materials. After years of reading and writing efforts inflicted by modern civilization, the individual develops a strong habit of deriving sound from a printed page, and this habit interferes with language learning. But it is only an acquired habit. The individual of college age has not lost forever the natural ability to connect sound with meaning, or conversely to derive meaning from sound without interposing a visual symbol of the sound. The Oklahoma experiment proved this. What a child can do so well before school has spoiled him, a man can still do later if wisely led. It is a matter of trying long enough with a short enough utterance. The utterance must be meaningful, of course, so that a concept is tied to the sounds. The success of the Oklahoma experiment lay in part in the briefness of the material. A single sentence of some twenty words and the fifty questions and answers that could be made up with those twenty words occupied the first week—five hours of class and about five hours of laboratory. And the second and third weeks' materials were not longer, only more difficult.

Every year, out of the twenty-five sections or so of first-year French students who are subjected to audio-lingual methods under our direction, a few come to our office and tell us in a most confidential tone something like this: "Sir, *I* am different. The others in the class seem to talk in French so easily. But I've got to see it in writing or I can't say it. Sir, may I have special permission to use a book in the lab?" We have never yielded. To persuade the student that he is not different, but perhaps only slower, we fire at him in quick succession some of the easy words and short utterances of the first-week material, and he soon realizes that he knows these completely, that they do evoke concepts without reference to any printed symbol.

2. Next in importance are the *physiological* habits of good pronunciation. These habits can be acquired much better and faster if the student does not see or visualize graphic forms at the same time. For every graphic form that a student sees, he has to combat the reflex of the articulatory movement corresponding to this letter in his native language. Our experience, for instance, is that any American student will produce a Parisian [R] in a few minutes by direct imitation of a native speaker of French (not of a record) if it is presented to him in a word he does not have a chance to see or visualize, such *carreau, aura, port, gare,* and if he does not have the least suspicion that the sound is spelled with an *r*. If a few minutes later the same student is shown the word in writing, the [r] reflex of his native language returns and causes his tongue tip to rise toward the palate and not to remain low as for [R]. In short, the interference of articulatory habits is enhanced by the graphic symbol.

In the Oklahoma experiment, new material was never presented on the record. It was always introduced first by the voice of the teacher, and practiced and corrected in class. The record was used to overlearn, to gain speed and fluency. There is no doubt that the first acquaintance with a new sound must be given (a) "live", so that the student can observe all that can be seen of the lips, tongue, jaws; (b) in slow motion, if necessary—the articulatory shortcuts of normal speed are features one is trained to hear and produce at a later stage; (c) with corrections on the part of the instructor—group repetition is never enough, each student must be heard individually and corrected at every class and day after day (this is why no more than twenty words per week can be learned properly at the start if there is only one instructor per class); (d) in meaningful utterances that will be expressed with appropriate prosodic features so that the key words which will later illustrate each phoneme may be remembered by complete concepts. Having learned new French sounds in French words, the audio-lingual students of the Oklahoma experiment never had to refer to English equivalents, either when they later read a printed page and had to be corrected, or when they learned the rules of French spelling. In both cases reference to key words they knew in French was sufficient.

In making points (a), (b), and (c), we are not trying to say that the teaching machine which dispenses with an instructor is an impossibility. If it does work, learning will take much longer than with initial human help, for the period of active production will have to be preceded by a long period of conditioning to the discrimination of aural stimuli. And since we understand the sounds of a new language not just by ear but by indirect reference to articulatory gestures of which we have already acquired the correct *habit* (speech psychologists have demonstrated this), it seems that the earlier we enter the production phase the better we can discriminate among the phonemes of a target language.

3. Finally, *grammatical* habits—that is, habits of correct morphology and syntax—must be acquired absolutely audio-lingually. The teaching of morphology, especially, must be done on the basis of how it sounds and not how it is written. In French more than in any other language, spelling is a mask behind which most of the reality of grammatical structure hides. It is not the *nt* of the spelling that distinguishes *il aime* from *ils aiment* but the alternation [l/z]: [ilɛm/ilzɛm]. It is not the *s* of the spelling that distinguishes *la table* from *les tables* but the alternation [a/e]: [latabl/letabl]. Spelling does not show whether or not a liaison occurs, or whether an unstable [ə] remains or falls. Commas and periods do not always indicate what intonation contours must be used, where the stresses must fall, how syllables must be separated. Not only does spelling fail to provide the true cues to morphology and syntax, it constantly gives false cues and spreads confusion. The only road to correct expression, in other words to grammatical habits, is by completely

audio-lingual contrastive drills using the techniques of addition, substitution and transformation. All this was understood and put into practice in the Oklahoma experiment.

Summary

Twenty years after the Oklahoma experiment, enormous technical advances have been made. The lone phonograph, around which students assembled in small groups to listen to scratchy stimuli and make responses in a whisper in order not to disturb the other listeners, is now replaced by the glorious modern language laboratory, a chapel of audio-lingual learning in which the devotees isolate themselves from the outside world and fervently commune with sound. But the principles on which the experiment was conceived and the precepts that were derived from it are firmly established. A program of audio-lingual teaching that will choose as its goal the three types of habits described above—psychological, physiological and grammatical—is bound to be successful.

CHAPTER II

A Model for Research in Programmed Self-instruction*

JOHN B. CARROLL
Harvard University

THE research described here is exploratory in nature. It does not pretend to give definitive answers, and it is by no means an experiment in the strict sense of the term. The intent was to see what could be done in Programmed Self-instruction (PSI) in a foreign language by use of the most practicable and well-designed techniques that could be devised in the light of the investigator's best knowledge and judgment. These techniques were to be shaped and modified, where it seemed wise, in the course of the investigation. There was no attempt to make any direct experimental comparisons of programmed instruction in a foreign language with other forms of instruction (for example, regular classroom instruction). Such comparisons are extremely difficult to make or to interpret. However, it is hoped that the results of the present investigation will speak for themselves in the sense of communicating what sort of outcome can be achieved in a carefully delineated learning situation.

Programmed Instruction

In a recent survey of programmed instruction in foreign languages (Carroll, 1963a), the author identified what he regarded as the

* Copyright © John B. Carroll.

three essential attributes of programmed instruction as it has developed in recent years:

1. Programmed instruction is based on a detailed psychological analysis of the objectives of the instruction. This analysis is put in terms of the "terminal behavior" which is sought in the learner as a result of the instruction.
2. The teaching materials and procedures used in programmed instruction reflect careful attention to the problem of sizing and sequencing of "steps". A "step" is a learning task which is presented and responded to in a confirmable manner before the learner proceeds. Steps are devised in such a size and in such sequential arrangement that the efficiency of learning and/or retention is optimal.
3. At each step, the learner is informed as to the correctness of his response. Programs of instruction are prepared in such a way that, if the learner's response is incorrect, there is a strong likelihood that he will be able to correct or improve his response when a suitable occasion for this response next appears.

This description of programmed instruction, it will be noted, is broad enough to apply to many types of instructional situations. For example, if the above criteria are met, a live teacher in a classroom will be offering programmed instruction. Because of the variation in learner response to instruction, however, programmed instruction is usually conducted in such a way that the learner can proceed at his own rate; this involves either individualized instruction (as with a private tutor) or self-instruction. In any case, the instruction is based on a program, i.e. a definite sequencing of instructional steps which is embodied, for example, in a written list, a series of printed question and answer "frames", a film, a magnetic tape, or some combination thereof. There is often (but not necessarily) some device for presenting the successive steps of the program and for informing the learner of the correctness of his responses at appropriate times (i.e., soon after the learner has made each confirmable response). This may be called a *presentation device*.

This paper is concerned with research only into programmed *self*-instruction (i.e. instruction in which a live instructor plays only a minimal role or no role at all, except, perhaps, in the original creation of the program).

Programmed Self-instruction in Foreign Languages

Investigation into the feasibility of programmed self-instruction in foreign languages is desirable for the following reasons:

1. Many languages exist which individuals desire to learn, or which, for one reason or another, it is desirable to teach, and these languages should be taught in the most efficient and effective manner possible.
2. Shortages prevail among competent instructors for many of these languages, and, in any case, in many situations self-instruction may be desirable.
3. It is possible that at least some aspects of foreign language instruction can be as effective in programmed instruction as in conventional classroom or individualized instruction, and perhaps more effective.

In the teaching of foreign languages, as in other subject areas, programmed instruction seems to offer a number of advantages over conventional instruction. Progress toward terminal competence can in theory be made faster, and this progress can be more controlled by the way in which instruction is programmed and presented.

In producing competence in the speaking and understanding of foreign languages (in contrast to reading and writing), programmed instruction will of necessity include auditory stimulation and overt spoken responses.* Instruction in "language laboratories" can be regarded as "programmed" if it meets the criteria previously set

* There have been attempts to program learning of foreign language phonology by solely visual means, i.e. without external auditory stimulation, but these attempts seem not only foolhardy (in view of the ease of providing recorded auditory stimulation) but also doomed to produce unsatisfactory results (because of the difficulty of shaping the articulations without an auditory model). No such attempt is made in the present investigation.

forth for programmed instruction, but it will not necessarily do so. With proper auditory or audio-visual presentation devices, programmed instruction should be able to take over much of the work of the foreign language teacher. In addition, an automated device can present instructional material tirelessly—at least up to the tolerance limit of the learner.

The live instructor seems to have two main advantages over any automated presentation device that can be conceived for at least the immediate future:

1. The live instructor can confirm the accuracy of the student's oral responses (and also of certain types of written responses, e.g. the writing of Chinese characters) more effectively and precisely than the student himself, even when the student has the opportunity to compare his response with a model response. One suspects that this limitation of self-instructional programs can be only partially overcome or compensated for by techniques of training the learner to make accurate evaluations of his own responses. (The current research made no use of such techniques, in order to see what could be accomplished without them.)

2. The live instructor can engage the student in free conversation. However, the absence of free conversation need not be considered a limitation of programmed self-instruction in foreign languages, any more than in a field like mathematics, where a program of self-instruction would not attempt to present the complete range of mathematical problems that a person might meet after completing the program. Free conversation may be regarded as an *application* of the terminal competence sought by an instructional program; it does not constitute the terminal competence itself. Terminal competence in a foreign language involves the ability to understand *any* sentence constructed according to the grammar and vocabulary of that language, and also the ability to construct or "generate" any proper sentence in that language. It is difficult to perceive any reason in principle why programmed instruction should not yield this kind of competence *without* use of a live instructor. Indeed, this may be regarded as a hypothesis of the present investigation.

Certain requirements in conducting research in programmed instruction in a foreign language seem fundamental. Above all is flexibility in the programming system and the manner of presentation. It was decided to construct a programming system and a presentation device which would allow as much flexibility as practical, because one would not want to specify in advance either the particular kinds of terminal behavior which one might eventually seek, or the particular format which one might eventually use. These desiderata included:

1. *Provision for audio-visual presentation*. Specifications of terminal behavior resulting from foreign language instruction are highly likely to include ability to respond to the *spoken* form of the language and competence in dealing with the *written* form of the language. The programming system must, therefore, incorporate means of presenting both auditory and visual modes of language. In addition, the system should be capable of presenting pictorial representations of objects, people, and situations to provide a referential basis for the instruction; the frame areas in which materials are to be presented must, therefore, be ample in size. While motion pictures might be desirable, it was felt that still pictures would be adequate for the present experiment. It was regarded as essential, however, that the audio and visual parts of the instruction should be intimately related and, to the maximum possible extent, presented simultaneously or in an integrated fashion. The completed instructional system thus contains provision for integrated auditory and visual presentations, the auditory signal coming from one channel of a two-track magnetic tape cartridge, and the visual information being presented by means of an image projected from a 35mm film strip.

2. *Provision for immediate confirmation of responses*. Regardless of whether "reinforcement" or reward is a critical element in learning, it is commonly agreed that amount of learning is often dependent upon the information the learner receives concerning the correctness of his responses. The program and its presentation must, therefore, be so arranged that every programmed response of the learner can

be confirmed or disconfirmed within a short time, usually only a few seconds.

3. *Provision for both multiple-choice and constructed responses, in any order.* It may be taken for granted that a large part of the terminal behavior sought in learning a foreign language consists of active, spontaneous responses "constructed" or "generated" by the speaker. At the same time, this terminal behavior also includes various kinds of *discriminative* responses, i.e. responses indicating which one of a number of possible alternatives is perceived. While it is true that these latter responses may be construed as free responses, there are indications that in programmed instruction it may be more efficient, and just as effective, to handle them as multiple-choice responses, i.e. responses in which the subject selects one of a number of alternatives. Furthermore, it is reasonable to suppose that a multiple-choice response is easier for the subject to make, and hence may be used as a preliminary to its elicitation in a free, "constructed" response. All the essential advantages of the multiple-choice response are present if provision is made for choice among five alternatives; therefore, it was decided to allow in the programming system a maximum of five alternatives per multiple-choice item. Provision was also made for a variety of free responses.

The recording and playback of the spoken responses might be desirable, for in this way the learner can listen to his spoken responses and examine them more attentively than he could otherwise. However, it was believed that this is not a great advantage, and since provision for it would have complicated the equipment, it was not allowed for in the present programmed instruction system. Nevertheless, care has been taken to provide that students receiving the auditory stimulus through headphones should also hear their own responses as spoken into a microphone. In this way the subject hears his spoken response approximately in the way he hears it in free air, i.e., with relatively little reliance on bone-conduction.

4. *Provision for repetition.* The terminal behaviors desired in foreign language learning may be more often characterized as skill behavior than as knowledge. The facile generation of a sentence in a foreign language is a very different thing from the mere knowledge

of *how* it should be constructed. A wealth of experience, in addition to psychological experiments on skill formation, suggests that fluency in a foreign language can be acquired only by generous amounts of repetition and overlearning.

One of the famous controversies in the field of programmed instruction has to do with whether a program should be linear or branching. However, this controversy has been carried on almost wholly in the context of instruction leading to *knowledge* rather than to facile skills and habits; further, it revolves almost wholly around the problem of whether error rate should be kept low and the problem of what to do about errors if they are made. This is not the issue here; rather, we are concerned about the problem of repetition and overlearning. But it may be pointed out that the conventional linear program, in which the learner goes through the program straight from frame 1 to frame N without any skips or retracings, can allow for repetition only by deliberate programming for it. In order for an item to be repeated, it must be included in a number of different frames distributed somehow throughout the program. This can lead to a certain amount of inefficiency in programming; at any rate it is likely to make the program inordinately lengthy, and if the length of the program is a factor in its cost, in its physical bulkiness, or in some other aspect, this sort of planned repetition may adversely affect acceptability.

It seemed desirable, therefore, to make a different kind of provision for repetition. In this respect, the kind of programmed instruction employed in the current project harks back to the principle of the memory drum, wherein a certain series of learning items is presented repetitively until a criterion is met. Since not all items are learned at the same rate, the repetition of a series may afford a good deal of overlearning of some items (i.e., learning beyond the point of meeting a criterion) while other items are being learned to a criterion. It is not necessary that repetition be made solely contingent on error rate, for repetition is probably desirable even when no errors have been made. But it is worth pointing out that learners can be more easily motivated to repeat material if they have made a certain number of errors. If the "overlearning" resulting from repetition is desirable, there is justification for writing a program at a level of difficulty such that at least a few errors are likely to occur. Furthermore, the learner's experience of a task in which he initially makes an error is likely to show him how he must modify his behavior in order to avoid a similar error in the future.

In this discussion one must be careful to observe what one means by the term "error". Usually, the term "error" refers to a response which is "incorrect", in the sense that whatever response is given does not match the "correct" response. It is usually argued that programs should be written so as to minimize this kind of error. But an "error" can also be a sheer absence of response, i.e. failure on the part of the learner to recall or construct *any* response which he feels will be acceptable. While it is perhaps inefficient to write programs in such a way that learners will frequently be at a loss to give any response, "errors" of this type at least are not subject to the objection that they are hard to eliminate once committed.

Provision for repetition was made by organizing the material into units of a size appropriate for repetition (called "loops"). The size of unit that was selected seems to work well; it is such that the normal "playing time" for the unit when it has been learned will be from 15 to 30 minutes. This is somewhat longer than the unit sometimes recommended for language laboratory exercises, that is, 5 minutes (Holton *et al.*, 1961, p. 194), but this comparison is inaccurate, for our units are more analogous to "the overall length of the laboratory lesson", described by Holton *et al.* as possibly varying "from 20 minutes to as much as 50 minutes". Such an organization of the program into repeatable units makes for a considerable degree of efficiency in programming and in the amount of material to be created. The programming technique used here may be called "cyclical", in contrast to the "linear" and "branching" techniques.

5. *Provision for branching.* To a large extent, repeatable loops take care of the problem of error by allowing the learner to repeat a loop until he has reduced his errors, if he makes them, to a satisfactory level. The repetition of a loop contingent upon a certain error rate could be said to be a variety of "branching", but in the

conventional parlance of programmed instruction "branching" usually implies that the student who "branches" is exposed to a *different* set of items or frames from the student who does not. Either he skips some items because of his superior performance, or he is routed to a series of remedial items because of his poor performance. This sort of branching could be utilized in the present programming system, if necessary, by providing different "loops" depending upon the learner's rate of progress; the unit, however, would be the loop rather than the individual frame. This kind of branching has not been used in the present study.

6. *Provision for "vanishing"*. In the normal course of learning, the learner is first presented with something which he is to learn, and, most often, he is supplied with a model of the response he is to make. At a later stage, the model is withdrawn and the learner is expected to make the response on his own. The process of withdrawing the model is sometimes called "vanishing"; the withdrawal can be gradual or sudden. In linear programs, the withdrawal takes place gradually over a series of frames, and the process can require lengthy programs if much attention is paid to it. In the present project, it was decided to provide for vanishing chiefly by means of a change in the "mode" of operation of the program. Three modes were possible: familiarization, learning, and testing. A student working with any given loop could experience first the familiarization mode (one or more times), next the learning mode (one or more times), and finally the testing mode.

Essentially, the familiarization mode presents the model of the response which is to be learned, while the learning mode presents the stimulus for the response without the response model. Thus, withdrawal is all-or-none rather than gradual. Nevertheless, the response model is sometimes available in the learning mode, i.e., it is available in a reduced form on request from the learner (in the form of a "prompt"). In the case of multiple-choice frames, it is also available as one of the alternative responses to be chosen, and in both the familiarization and the learning modes the subject can try one alternative after another, if he wishes, to arrive at the correct response. (However, the count of the learner's errors depends solely on the first response he makes; that is, only his first response is counted right or wrong, as the case may be.)

7. *Provision for satisfactory "human engineering" of the learning environment.* The writer feels that such presentation devices as programmed textbooks and teaching machines such as the Koncept-o-graph (for example) require too many irrelevant and onerous manual responses—frequent page-turning, careful turning of knobs to bring new program material into view in precisely the correct framing, etc. It was therefore decided to design the presentation device in such a way that operation would be as simple and easy as possible; thus, the learner operates the machine solely by pushing buttons or throwing switches. The buttons used most frequently contain lights which light up when they can be legitimately operated. Further, the experimental booth and the presentation device were designed and laid out so as to maximize comfort and minimize fatigue and strain.

8. *Provision for adequate control or guidance of the learner's attention.* In any system of programmed instruction, it is desirable to control the learner's attention as closely as possible. At any given moment, the particular visual stimulus to which the learner is to attend should be clearly identified, and there must be adequate alerting to auditory signals. At the same time, certain kinds of programming may require that the learner have available a range of visual stimuli, so that he can make comparisons and contrasts.

In the case of the present programming system, these desiderata have been provided for by:

(a) having the visual stimuli appear on a rear projection screen such that the experimental room must be at least partially darkened in order that the images may be seen clearly, with the result that the images on the screen acquire saliency over surrounding visual stimuli;
(b) presenting visual images in different parts of a frame at different times, by means of a shutter arrangement;
(c) having the shutters expose materials immediately after a button-push by the subject (so that the button-push is an

FIG. 1. Front view of the automated audio-visual instructional device, AVID. A sample film loop is resting on top of the box containing the projection screen; a sample magnetic tape cartridge is resting against the wall of the same box *(center right)*. To the left of the projection screen are *(above)* a small loudspeaker and *(below)* a box containing relays and auxiliary controls; in the foreground is the control panel operated by the student and *(bottom right)* the write-in paper tape. See Fig. 3 for further explanation.

operant leading to the visual image—insofar as the visual image is a secondary reinforcer—motivating the desired observing behavior);

(d) having auditory stimulation occur immediately after a button-press (so that the button-press simultaneously acts as an operant leading to auditory material, motivating listening behavior);

(e) sequencing the opening of the shutters so that during some phases of the work with a given frame, the learner is exposed not only to new material but at the same time has available a visual stimulus seen earlier; this allows the learner to compare new material with previously seen material. See Fig. 1.

9. *Provision for self-pacing*. It is perhaps not completely evident from the foregoing that the presentation must be paced by the learner. This is thought to be desirable for the following reasons:

(a) Learners probably vary in the amount of time they need to spend in observing and responding to each segment of a program.
(b) Programmers find it difficult to specify in advance how much time even an average subject will need to complete any segment of the program. Any automatic pacing specified in advance is therefore likely to lead to incomplete or inefficient learning.

The pacing of the present programmed instruction system is almost completely under the control of the learner. The learner can view each *visual* segment for as long or as short a time as he desires, and he can wait as long as he wishes between *auditory* segments of the program; he can even interrupt (stop) an auditory presentation. The only limitation is that during any given "trip" through a loop, the subject can listen to any given segment of auditory program only once. Future versions of the presentation device, it is planned, will include an arrangement whereby the learner can replay a segment of an auditory presentation.

A Research Project in PSI

Scope of the Study

For several reasons, Mandarin Chinese was selected as the language to be taught:

1. Mandarin Chinese is so different from any of the Western languages which American students are likely to have studied that the question of facilitation or interference in prior language study could safely be ignored in connection with the recruiting of subjects for the experiment. Further, it would be easy to find students whose knowledge of Mandarin Chinese at the start of training was effectively zero.
2. Spoken Mandarin Chinese possesses a number of characteristics which present a special challenge for self-instructional programming, for example, the tone system and certain aspects of the syntax. At the same time, spoken Chinese is generally regarded as a language which is not inordinately difficult to learn.
3. Undoubtedly the most difficult aspect of Chinese is the use of Chinese characters. It was felt that these difficulties would make Chinese particularly appropriate for adaptation in a course utilizing an audio-*visual* machine.
4. Excellent materials were already available for conventional instruction in Chinese, and these materials have been successfully used at a number of institutions. It was thus deemed satisfactory to develop the self-instructional program on the basis of the plan of linguistic analysis utilized in these materials. Also, a basis of comparison with outcomes of conventional instruction was available if desired.

The intention was to program an amount of Mandarin Chinese instruction which would be approximately equivalent to 1 month of intensive instruction as conducted, for example, at the Institute of Far Eastern Languages (IFEL) at Yale University, or to one semester's work in a regular college course.

Specifically, the program was designed to teach essentially all of the material of the first nine lessons of the textbook *Speak Chinese*, by M. G. Tewksbury (1948), and the first fifty characters introduced in the textbook *Read Chinese*, by F-Y Wang (1953). Both texts are published by IFEL. At IFEL, about 2½ lessons of *Speak Chinese* are covered in a week of intensive instruction; about 2 months are taken to cover all twenty-four lessons of it.

By choosing to build a self-instructional program on the basis of an already fixed textbook presentation, one may lose a certain degree of flexibility in exploiting the possible advantages of programmed instruction. Furthermore, one is forced to accept, in large measure, the assumptions about foreign language teaching which underlie the text selected for adaptation. For example, Tewksbury's *Speak Chinese* is patterned on the so-called "Army method" of foreign language instruction and makes liberal use of translation; i.e. every new linguistic item is introduced with an English translation, and some of the exercises are based on translation. Some foreign language teachers feel that translation should be used as sparingly as possible, if at all; they feel that meanings should be introduced by means of pictorial referents, gestures, or verbal context. Nevertheless, programming in order to avoid translation would probably have meant a complete reworking of the design of the language course, because many of the items introduced in early stages of Tewksbury's *Speak Chinese* cannot be easily suggested by pictorial or context means.

In any case, the evidence for eschewing translation is not at all clear. Fernand Marty (1962, p. 65) reports that a method which avoided translation did not prove satisfactory, largely because it was inefficient. Too much time was taken up in trying to convey meanings, and doing it poorly; the student did not have the illusion of generating new sentences when he was simply asked to do substitution drills. Further, retention was poorer for material learned by substitution drill.

The view was taken, therefore, that for the present study it would be satisfactory to make a rather straightforward adaptation of the Tewksbury textbook as it stood, including the use of translation.

The straightforward adaptation of conventional text materials into the form of programmed instruction may be termed "expediency programming". Expediency programming is probably easier and less demanding than more advanced forms of programming, and may make it economically feasible to program a large number of "neglected" languages. There is not as yet any evidence as to the relative efficiency of programs constructed by "expediency programming" as compared with programs devised along allegedly more sophisticated lines.

The terminal behaviors desired by our program can be summarized as follows:

1. Ability to discriminate the phonemes of the language and to transcribe them with high accuracy in a uniform system of phonemic transcription.
2. Ability to speak words and phrases with a good approximation to the rendition of a native speaker, exhibiting the ability to make all the phonemic distinctions in the language.
3. Recognition of the lexical and grammatical meanings of some 159 Chinese words, and ability to speak and write these words (phonemic transcription is meant here).
4. Recognition of the grammatical meanings of about thirty-five syntactical patterns.
5. Ability to comprehend novel sentences constructed with the forms and words presented in the program, and to demonstrate this ability by accurate translation into English.
6. Ability to utter novel sentences using the syntactical patterns and words presented in the program, and to demonstrate this ability by accurate translation of English into Chinese.
7. Ability to recognize fifty Chinese characters as corresponding to their equivalents in the spoken language; also, ability to *copy* these characters with correct stroke order (but not necessarily to write them without a model, although this is taught incidentally in the program as an aid to memorization).

A considerable variety of programming techniques were used. This was possible partly because of the great flexibility of the presentation device. Some programming principles used are the following:

1. Wherever possible, the student should be advised, in advance, of how much he is going to learn, and exactly what aspects of the materials he is to learn. For example, in the first two frames of the first loop he is told that there are four tones in Mandarin Chinese and that he must learn the numbers for these tones and the way in which they are transcribed in the transcription system used in the program.

2. Instructions play an important role in directing learning. For example, in an early frame the student is told to pay attention "mainly to the sound" of the several Chinese words to be presented, whereas twenty frames later he is told to pay attention to their meanings.

3. Unless attention is being directed to particular aspects of linguistic forms or symbols, foreign language material to be learned should be presented, insofar as possible, in complete utterances, however short they may be. The material should be presented in contrasting patterns so that the learner can easily infer what part of each pattern has a given significance. It is believed that if this procedure is followed, it is safe to present many aspects of foreign language materials essentially as paired-associate learning tasks. If possible, pairing should be between a foreign language word and an actual or pictured referent; but a native-language approximate translation equivalent may serve as the key to the meaning. Continued practice in giving English for Chinese or Chinese for English will lead to automatization of response. Practice in comprehension of rapid spoken Chinese will facilitate the virtual dropping out of native-language mediating responses.

4. Discrimination training should involve close juxtaposition of similar but confusable items so that the learner can observe the differences between the items. For example, the difference in tone between *mǎi* "buy" and *mài* "sell" is pointed out and tested; and later, distinctions in meaning among *kéyi*, *hwèi*, and *néng* are pointed out and tested.

5. Possible influences of negative transfer from prior learning should be carefully pointed out so that the learner may avoid them. For example, one frame deals with the sound of the letter *e* in the

transcription. However, the results showed that this was by no means enough warning to the students, since many of them continued to pronounce this letter with the phoneme [e] rather than [ə].

Special Problems in Programming Aspects of the Chinese Language

1. *Phonology.* It was decided to begin the program with a presentation of the four Chinese tones, on a variety of syllables which would offer no difficulty phonemically. The program makes the student aware that there are four tones in Chinese which are important in carrying differences in meaning, and that he has to learn to discriminate among them, produce them, and know the numbers and diacritical marks assigned to them. It was assumed that learning the tone differences would be facilitated if the student was made cognitively aware of the differences in their tonal contours; these contours are conveyed by quasi-musical notation. In the first loop, the learner is asked first to imitate the several tones (three frames), then to recognize the tones and indicate their numbers (next four frames), and then to produce them and compare his own production with a model provided in the answer-phase. Considerable attention is paid to tones in later parts of the program (e.g., in the first loop of Lesson II, the student is asked to write new vocabulary with proper transcription and diacritical marks).

In connection with some of the segmental phonemes, considerable explanation is given in terms of manner of articulation and other phonetic aspects; many students are able to profit from these explanations. At the same time, practice is given in identifying and discriminating phonemes.

In general, the assumption was made that most students would in time learn to recognize and imitate Chinese sounds with reasonable accuracy, merely through practice in discriminating them, and through the opportunity to compare oral productions with a model, and to study explanations in terms of articulatory phonetics. The results showed that this assumption was largely correct; in the few instances in which students failed to acquire proper phonemic discriminative and oral responses, it was evident that the program had failed to give enough attention to the features involved.

2. *Vocabulary.* Because of the limited vocabulary employed and the fact that most of the vocabulary items are supplied with fairly close English equivalents, there seemed to be little difficulty in the teaching of vocabulary. Pictorial materials are little used because of the added effort and expense that would have been involved, although illustrations are introduced in a few frames to show what can be done. A conscious effort is made to repeat each vocabulary item, once introduced, enough times in new contexts to insure learning. Test results showed that there were very few instances in which a subject failed to learn vocabulary equivalents (either Chinese in response to English, or vice-versa).

3. *Grammar.* The rationale underlying the presentation of grammatical materials included the following ideas: (a) each grammatical pattern or transformation must be introduced as a separate entity to be learned and thoroughly exemplified before sentences exemplifying new patterns are introduced; (b) the "dynamic logic" of a particular grammatical pattern should be evident in the pattern itself and the way it is used, and particularly in contrast to patterns previously introduced; (c) grammatical explanations or other comments on patterns should be used *after* the patterns have been exemplified, in order to help the learner to organize cognitively the structure of the language he is learning; (d) the learner should be required to practice grammatical transformations, translations, and other manipulations of grammatical patterns, this sort of practice being in general better than the mere repetition of grammatical patterns.

4. *Graphemes.* Chinese characters are introduced to the learner in the first loop of Lesson V. He is first taught the basic strokes composing characters and given practice in making these strokes, at first alone, then as parts of easy characters. Certain rules and generalizations are stated concerning the order in which the strokes of a Chinese character are to be made, and the learner is given practice in following these rules in successively more complicated and involved characters. The first set of characters which the learner has to memorize is the set of characters for the digits 1 to 10.

In the next loop, he learns ten fairly simple characters, each representing a word already learned in its spoken counterpart. The technique of teaching is extremely simple: in the presentation phase, the learner is shown the character, with the stroke order indicated, and told to learn it. He tests himself in the question and answer phases. The answer area makes use of the "rebus method" introduced in the textbook *Read Chinese* (Wang, 1953), which provides for a gradual introduction of Chinese characters interspersed in phonemic transcription.

5. *Aural comprehension.* Because a great deal of the program is presented auditorily, there is much opportunity for practice in aural comprehension. Many frames require the student to listen to a Chinese sentence and translate it, answer questions on it, or perform some grammatical transformation on it. In some loops, there is a deliberate attempt to present spoken Chinese at a fairly rapid pace; in the presentation phase the student can accustom himself to listening to Chinese at this pace, and in the question and answer phases he tests his aural comprehension. Generally, such aural comprehension drills occur in the later loops of a lesson, often just before the dialogue which is to be learned in each lesson except the first.

6. *Oral production.* The learner gets continual practice in producing sentences of increasing complexity utilizing the grammar and vocabulary he has learned up to any given point. Cues for sentence production are provided either by English sentences to be translated or by Chinese sentences to be responded to in some way. The English sentence is by all odds the most reliable way of cueing sentence generation; although it may seem to have the disadvantage of permitting a compound type of bilingualism it seems to be the most efficient way of eliciting a particular kind of sentence response in a foreign language, for it corresponds in some way to the process by which a speaker would generate a sentence in a real-life situation in speaking a foreign language. That is to say, the English sentences which are provided to the learner are "imitations" of the kind of "thought" that precedes the generation of a sentence in a foreign-language speaking situation.

Two special techniques for programming oral production may deserve notice. One is the "timed oral response" technique. In the question phase, the learner is given a task to perform before the answer occurs on the tape, some definite number of seconds after the start of the question phase. The subject must therefore not only give the correct response, but also give it within a certain time period. This technique can also be utilized in the presentation phase.

The other special technique is the teaching of a dialogue. Dialogues give practice in both aural comprehension and oral production. The programming system makes it possible for the learner, after he has learned his part of a dialogue, almost to have the illusion of "talking" to an interlocutor on the tape. The learner is supposed to learn both parts of a dialogue: if the two speakers in a dialogue are called A and B, he first learns to listen to A's part and make B's responses, after which he learns to listen to B's part and give A's responses. Learning the dialogue occurs in the familiarization mode; the illusion of actually participating in a dialogue occurs in the learning mode, where the two parts can follow each other in close succession, alternating between question phase and answer phase. See Fig. 2.

The loops contain a wide variety of programming techniques not only because a rather diverse set of skills have to be taught but also because in this way it was hoped that boredom and fatigue could be minimized. Learners seemed to look forward to each new loop with curiosity and favorable anticipation.

In the process of traversing loops repeatedly, it was realized that subjects would sometimes learn irrelevant facts related to the position of the response. For example, after several repetitions the learner might remember that the answer to a given problem is response button No. 4, without also remembering what the answer is. The degree to which this occurs cannot be assessed, nor can any statement be made as to whether such learning is beneficial or deleterious. It could be argued that it is beneficial in the sense that getting right answers easily (even though "illegally") may be rewarding and smooth the way of the learner. In any event, an attempt was made to provide enough instances of each item to be learned so that subjects could rely on irrelevant cues to a minimal extent.

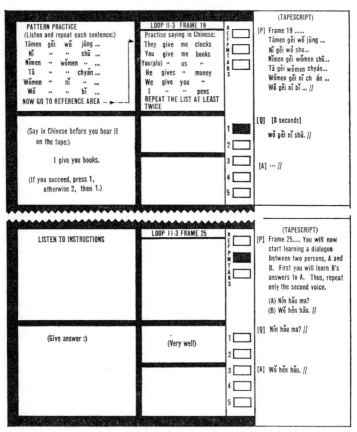

FIG. 2. Sample frames from self-instructional program in Mandarin Chinese.

Summary and Recommendations

The presentation device, or teaching machine, is designed and constructed to serve what are believed to be the special requirements of programmed self-instruction in spoken and written foreign languages. Chief of these special requirements are: (1) correlated audio-visual stimulation, and (2) provision for repetition of stimuli and responses with progressive reduction of the prompting of responses. In addition, the device had to provide for various standard features of programmed instruction such as immediate confirmation of responses and self-pacing. These and other requirements (economy, convenience, durability, etc.) dictated the development of a prototype teaching machine utilizing loops of 35mm strip film and standard magnetic tape as the media on which the instructional materials are recorded. The design also provides a fairly complicated logic circuitry to make possible the presentation of synchronized audio-visual materials in three modes (familiarization, learning, and testing), with various modes of student response (multiple choice or free response by speaking or by writing). The design allows the use of linear programs and also certain types of branching programs, but the type of program to which it is especially adapted may be called "cyclical", for the student can work with each loop as many times in each presentation mode as necessary to achieve a desired degree of mastery. The presentation modes differ principally in the degree to which the responses are prompted; in the familiarization mode, for example, new information can be supplied in every frame, and prompting of responses can be as direct as desired. In the learning mode, it is assumed that new items to be learned have already been presented, and the prompting of the responses is therefore much less direct or eliminated altogether. The testing mode (not actually used in the experimentation reported here) differs from the learning mode only in that there is no confirmation of responses provided.

To test the feasibility of the audio-visual presentation device and the associated programming system, a 936-frame program designed to teach certain introductory phases of spoken and written Mandarin Chinese was prepared. The terminal behavior desired was described in detail. The program itself was adapted from existing instructional materials in Mandarin Chinese, and presented an amount of material which is equivalent approximately to that presented in one month (about 90 hours) of intensive language instruction at the Institute of Far Eastern Languages, Yale University. A wide variety of programming techniques was used in order to explore the feasibility of automated teaching of various aspects of language skills such as phonemic discrimination and production, vocabulary learning, acquisition of grammatical patterns, practice of dialogues, and learning to recognize and write Chinese characters. Quantitatively, the program can be described as presenting all the phonemes of Mandarin Chinese, the Yale Romanized transcriptions for these phonemes, 159 vocabulary items, thirty-five grammatical structures or grammar points, and fifty Chinese characters.

Experimental work proceeded in two phases. Experiment I, conducted in the summer of 1961, utilized eight volunteer subjects of college age or above and of varying language aptitude who were put through the first six loops of the twenty-two-loop program in either "massed" or "spaced" trial schedules. This experiment disclosed that the massing or spacing of the trials made no appreciable difference in student performance. It appeared to indicate that the machine and the program were designed in a generally satisfactory manner, but that the "ground rules" under which the subjects were to perform their work were of critical importance. In Experiment I, subjects were required to repeat each loop in both the familiarization and the learning modes until they reduced their errors to 10% or less. The learners objected strenuously to this requirement, claiming that error rate was not a completely reliable index to degree of learning and pointing out that trying to meet a given error rate was both frustrating and distracting. Therefore, a second experiment, utilizing fifteen students of college age and above, was conducted with changed "ground rules". In the latter experiment, carried out in the academic year 1961–62 and the summer of 1962, subjects were allowed to proceed through the program with as few or as many repetitions as they liked, provided they performed each loop once in the familiarization mode and once in the learning mode. See Fig. 3.

This procedure was found to be satisfactory; performance of subjects in the program was not attended with the degree of

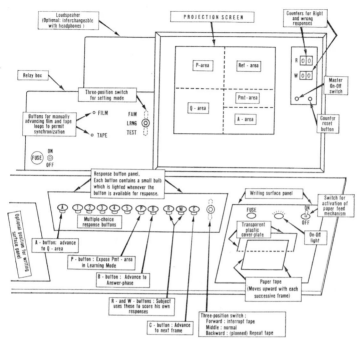

Fig. 3. Layout of console for AVID, experimental teaching machine.

frustration and emotional disturbance that was evident in the earlier experiment.

In both experiments, measures of language aptitude, performance in the program, and performance on criterion tests were taken. The small number of subjects in the first experiment made it difficult to draw any reliable conclusions except that all subjects evidenced a high degree of learning on criterion tests; the rates at which subjects progressed through the program varied considerably. With fifteen subjects in the second experiment, significant correlations were obtained between various measures of aptitude, program performance, and final achievement. On criterion tests, achievement ranged from approximately 65% to nearly 100%, but achievement was strongly correlated with language aptitude and with rate of progress through the program. Rates of progress varied by as much as a factor of three or four. The results suggested that the structure of the program permits highly efficient learning for high aptitude students, but demands much time and attention from low aptitude students. Since very little attempt was made, in the present research, to modify or revise the program that was written, or to submit such modifications to further field trials, no conclusions can be drawn concerning whether program revisions would permit easier or more efficient learning for low aptitude students.

Tentative answers may be given to the questions posed at the outset of this investigation:

1. *To what extent, and how well, can skill and competence in a foreign language be attained purely by programmed self-instruction (PSI) without the aid of an instructor?* It is evident from the experiments conducted thus far that many aspects of foreign language skill and competence can indeed be attained by programmed self-instruction. If the criterion tests devised in the present research are accepted as representing the types of skills desired in foreign language instruction, this research presents exact data on the extent to which these skills were achieved through the programmed self-instruction offered to the students in the field trials. Some students achieved nearly perfect scores on these tests.

2. *Can some aspects of foreign language competence be better taught by PSI than others, and if so, what are these aspects?* This question now seems essentially unanswerable because it assumes that different aspects of foreign language performance can be measured on a comparable basis. If the question is rephrased to ask whether there are any aspects of foreign language competence that cannot be taught by PSI, a meaningful answer can be given. From the evidence collected here, it would seem that there are *no* aspects of foreign language competence that cannot be taught at least to some degree by PSI. The program and the programming system devised here were successful to a considerable degree in teaching accurate phonemic discrimination, phoneme production, ability to use a transcription system, knowledge of vocabulary, production of

grammatically accurate sentences both in speech and writing, comprehension of sentences spoken at a normally fast rate of speed, and reading and writing of Chinese characters. This research has disclosed no evidence that would suggest that some aspects of foreign language competence *cannot* be produced by PSI; rather, the failure to produce complete competence can be most immediately attributed to shortcomings in the writing of the program. For example, not all students learned phonemic discriminations and phoneme production as accurately as might have been desired. Probably, this was due to an overestimation on the part of the investigator of the ability of students to learn these behaviors and a consequent underemphasis of these aspects in the program. Another example of a program shortcoming was the failure to give enough separate attention to the learning of the tone associated with each new Chinese word introduced.

At present, this investigator feels that further efforts should be made to develop programs that will teach all desired aspects of foreign language performance. The present program in Mandarin Chinese could in all probability be modified to the point where it would be satisfactory in this respect. Only if such efforts ultimately fail can we conclude that some aspects of foreign language performance cannot be successfully taught by PSI.

3. *To what extent can an automated audio-visual presentation device aid in teaching foreign language skills?* It is inconceivable that the success achieved in the present experiment could have been achieved without some sort of audio-visual presentation, at least the kind of presentation that could be made by an ordinary tape recorder correlated with the visual presentation afforded by, let us say, a "programmed text". It is difficult to state, however, how much the rather complicated device employed in the present experiment enhanced its success by making learning more convenient and better controlled for the subjects. Certainly, the presentation of the program with the various frame areas exposed at the right times, with auditory presentations properly paced and with confirmations accurately meted out, would be difficult to accomplish with much more limited electromechanical resources.

At any rate, for reasons of economy, efforts should be made to see how much the present audio-visual presentation device can be simplified or modified without too great a sacrifice of its many worthwhile features; e.g. the use of microfilm for visual presentation rather than paper and the consequent economy of production and storage, the use of the same program material in different ways (i.e. "learning modes") and the consequent economy both in programming and information storage, and the use of automatic confirmation of responses.

4. *What are the most effective and acceptable ways of programming self-instruction in a foreign language?* The present research was not designed to provide answers to detailed questions concerning programming techniques. It can be asserted with considerable confidence that the programming techniques devised and employed in this research were reasonably effective. It is believed, too, that the "cyclical" programming system developed here made for considerable efficiency both in programming and in learning—more efficiency, that is, than would have been attained by a purely linear program. The occasionally high error rates encountered as learners work through the initial stages of a program are not as objectionable, apparently, as some writers on programmed instruction have believed. Learners do not resist the challenge of a task which is difficult but whose difficulty they know to be surmountable.

5. *What are students' rates of progress under PSI, and what levels of competence can be achieved after various periods of time under PSI?* It is difficult to make generalizations concerning rates of progress. It is believed that the data amassed here will be useful as providing a set of baselines for evaluating other programs or modes of instruction. As has been stated above, students *do* learn under PSI; if they take a sufficient amount of time, even low aptitude students approach satisfactory levels of performance. On the average, students appear to progress about twice as fast as they do under conventional intensive instruction in the classroom. It is possible that with program revision, rates of progress would be even faster.

6. *How are students' rates of progress under PSI related to their aptitude for learning foreign languages and to other variables?* There

are indications from our research that rate of learning is highly correlated with aptitude for learning a foreign language as measured by the Carroll–Sapon *Modern Language Aptitude Test* (1958–1959). This tends to confirm the writer's hypothesis (Carroll, (1963b)) that aptitude is essentially a matter of time required for learning. On the other hand, it is possible that the correlation observed between foreign language aptitude and rate of progress was partly a function of some characteristic of the program, such as its difficulty. The present research did not disclose any other background variable that was significantly related to rate of progress in PSI; all the students appeared to be well motivated.

7. *What are students' reactions to PSI in a foreign language?* The comments of the students employed in the experiments reported here were in general highly favorable to programmed self-instruction in foreign languages. They enjoyed this form of learning, on the whole, even though it was occasionally frustrating and boring. Frustrations and boredom were perceived as more the fault of particular conditions (poor programming, carelessness on the part of the learner, machine failures, etc.) than of programmed instruction as such. It is difficult to know to what extent these comments were biased by the fact that the subjects in the experiment were essentially volunteers, all with some considerable degree of motivation either to learn Chinese or to experience programmed instruction.

8. *What factors of cost, acceptability, efficiency of learning, and so forth, need to be considered in the assessment of PSI as a mode of teaching foreign languages, whether or not it is used in conjunction with regular classroom or individual teaching by a live instructor?* Matters of acceptability and of efficiency of learning having already been covered above, problems of cost remain to be discussed. Here it is necessary to be quite frank. Programmed self-instruction involves rather large outlays of money, particularly in the development phases.

Engineering costs incurred in the acquisition and development of the two prototype models of the audio-visual presentation device used in this experiment (AVID) were approximately $10,000.

It may be estimated that production models of this device cannot be made for much less than $1000 each unless they are made in large quantities. In any event, the device should be redesigned rather completely before it is made in any large quantities, entailing further engineering costs which might range between $10,000 and $50,000. Ultimately, it might be possible to produce commercially a somewhat simplified and redesigned version of AVID for $300–500 apiece; exactly how much more than this would be a feasible sales price is difficult to say at this time. In any event, the kind of audio-visual presentation device which seems desirable for PSI in foreign languages will be fairly expensive. On the other hand, this expense may not be, in the long run, much greater than the expense presently incurred by many school systems in the installation of foreign language laboratories, and the learning attainable through PSI may be much greater and more efficient.

The other principal factor of cost is the cost of developing and producing programs. Certain cost estimates can be made on the basis of experience acquired during the present research. These are *net* development and production costs, rather conservatively estimated, and do not include overhead, travel, training, research, and other related costs. They are simply the costs that the investigator estimates he would incur if requested to prepare additional program materials similar to those already prepared for this research. They are estimated on the basis of the programming system as it evolved in the course of this research after a number of false starts, experiences with inefficient procedures, etc., that have not been detailed here.

The estimates are of the cost of producing one "frame" in the present programming system. It should be recognized that the "frame" utilized in this system is more elaborate and is presented more times to the learner than the "frame" of the usual "linear" program. In fact, it may be estimated that for each frame of the present programming system, from five to ten frames would be used in a conventional linear program covering the same material.

Our experience is that about 100 frames are needed to cover the material of a typical lesson in a standard foreign language textbook. The average number of lessons presented in such a textbook, suitable for a 1-year standard college course, or for 12 weeks of intensive instruction, is about thirty. Therefore, it may be estimated that 3000 frames would be needed to cover the material for an introductory language course. Thus the following per frame estimates should be multiplied by 3000 to obtain total cost of a programmed foreign language course.

Our estimates are based on the assumption that instructional materials (textbooks, grammars, etc.) already exist that can be adapted for programmed instruction by persons competent to do so. The programmers used in the present research were either experienced teachers of Chinese or (in the case of the writer) a psycholinguist with extensive experience in linguistics and language learning.

Program Development Costs (per frame)

	$
Programmer time to plan and write the frame (30 minutes, at $5·00 per hour)	2·50
Supervision and review (10 minutes, at $6·25 per hour)	1·04
Typing of frame on a standard form for camera copy, including accompanying tapescript, with proofreading and checking (20 minutes per frame, at $2·10 per hour)	0·70
Cost of filming from camera copy, including labor and materials	0·10
Cost of making master tape (labor and materials) (including native speaker, engineer, etc.)	0·25
Cost of making required copies of master tape and packaging in cartridges, including labor and materials (one familiarization tape, one learning tape)	0·15
Total per-frame cost for materials ready for tryout in AVID	$ 4·74
Total cost for 1 loop, forty frames	$189·60

Program Reproduction Costs (per frame)

	$
Filming from camera copy	0·10
Production of a familiarization mode tape and a learning mode tape, in cartridges	0·15
Total per-frame cost for one extra set of materials	$ 0·25
Total cost for 1 loop, forty frames	$10·00

Thus, it may be estimated that the total cost of the 22-loop program developed for this research was $4171·20; the set of extra copies that was made represented an outlay of $220·00.

All these costs are prior to program tryout and revision. If unpaid volunteers are used in program tryout, the cost would be about $0·33 per frame on the following assumptions: that ten subjects are used, that each subject spends an average of 2·5 minutes per frame, that the supervisor is paid at the rate of $1·60 per hour, and that two subjects are run simultaneously. We have no data pertinent to the cost of program revision, but many of the costs of initial programs development would recur in program revision. Further, there would be the cost of analyzing data from the initial tryout. It may be estimated that the cost of program revision would not be less than half that of initial program development, that is, $2·37 per frame. To recapitulate the estimated costs for revised program:

	$
Cost of initial development (per frame)	4·74
Extra copy of program for tryout (per frame)	0·25
Cost of tryout of initial program (per frame)	0·33
Data analysis and program revision (per frame)	2·37
Extra copy of revised program for tryout (per frame)	0·25
Cost of tryout of revised program (per frame)	0·33
Data analysis, compilation of data (per frame)	0·50
Total cost, revised program (per frame)	$8·77

If this cost is multiplied by 3000, the estimated number of frames required for a standard introductory course in a language, the resulting figure is $26,310. Each extra copy of the program material would cost $750 if produced by the techniques worked out in the present project; some economies could probably be effected, however, if copies were mass-produced and materials such as cartridges were acquired at more favorable discount prices than were encountered.

While the above costs may seem rather large, they must be evaluated in comparison with the cost of conventional instruction using live instructors. The above program costs are for the most part nonrecurrent; sets of program materials could be re-used an indefinite number of times. The cost of programmed self-instruction, therefore, would decrease markedly with the number of students using it, as Kopstein and Cave (1962) found in a study of programmed instruction in the Air Force.

In view of the cost of developing material for programmed self-instruction in a foreign language, projects for such development should not be undertaken lightly. The above estimates of costs are on the conservative side, and do not allow for the profits that would be reasonably expected in a commercial enterprise or even the overhead that would have to be charged by a nonprofit organization.

It may also be remarked that effective development, production, and tryout of programs requires the gathering together of a competent and well organized group of personnel. In addition to the person supervising the operation, the following types of persons are required:

Programmers: Obviously, programmers must be familiar with the language to be taught, either as native speakers of it or as persons who have learned it quite thoroughly. In addition, they must be able to write effective English. They must also be familiar with principles and techniques of programming; our experience, however, is that this familiarity can be acquired quite rapidly.

Clerical workers: Clerical workers are needed for typing program material on special formats for camera copy, often with exacting problems of layout, special characters, diacritical marks, etc.; also for analysis of data from tryouts, typing reports, etc.

Technicians: Several different types of skills are needed; sometimes they are found in a single person. First, photographic skill is needed in setting up the camera, making films, developing them, and splicing them into loops. Second, competence in tape-recording techniques is needed for engineering the production of master tapes and the copying of masters into endless-loop tape cartridges. Third, competence in simple electronic and mechanical repairs is needed for the maintenance of audio-visual presentation devices and associated equipment.

Artists: If pictorial material is to be used in the visual presentations, an artist may be required to make suitable line drawings. (The use of such materials in the present project was extremely limited and should be increased in future work.)

Native informants and speakers: Someone born to the language is needed for checking over program material, for voicing foreign language material on tape, and for writing special characters or script for camera copy. Also, preparation of the master tape requires a person with a good speaking voice and good English diction.

Tryout supervisors: Supervisors are needed to schedule and supervise volunteer subjects during tryouts of the program material.

Despite the costs and the still unsolved problems, the eventual benefits from programmed self-instruction in foreign languages appear very promising and worthwhile, in the opinion of the present writer.

Future Directions

If programmed self-instruction in foreign languages is to be successfully undertaken, the following future directions for research and development need special attention:

1. *Refinement of programming techniques.* A host of interesting and

fruitful problems for research presented themselves in the course of the present investigation. Most of these problems were by-passed or laid aside in the development of the program, since it was necessary to assume tentative solutions. Among the most interesting problems are: What are the best techniques for teaching phonemic discrimination? What techniques are available for teaching accurate phonemic production in the absence of a live instructor? At what rate should new items be introduced? How much review and repetition of previously introduced items is desirable? What are the most effective kinds of practice to insure mastery of grammatical patterns? At what rate should prompts and cues to responses be "vanished"? How rapidly can auditory material be speeded up and still be within the auditory comprehension speed of the learner? What aspects of foreign language learning present most difficulty for low aptitude students, and how can programs be adapted to the needs of such students?

2. *Partial mechanization of the production of programs.* In view of the enormous labor in laying out and writing programs, a partial mechanization of this process, possibly through the use of high-speed computers, would be desirable. There is a distinct possibility that computers could be programmed to accept coded information concerning the phonology, structure, and lexicon of the language to be taught and on this basis lay out a skeleton of a program that could then be "fleshed out" and refined by competent teaching-machine programmers. For example, vocabulary items could be introduced and repeated at controlled rates, and the same might be true of grammatical and phonological items.

3. *Simplification and refinement of audio-visual presentation devices.* The prototype audio-visual presentation devices developed for this research presented many difficulties. They lacked a satisfactory degree of sturdiness and reliability, and they were not easy to use because insertion of program material (film and tape loops) was inconvenient, time-consuming, and delicate. A thorough redesign of the equipment will be necessary to solve these difficulties. The suggestions made by Waite (1963) concerning audio-visual teaching machines might be of value. In addition, some aspects of

the programming system might be simplified. For example, so little use was made of the "prompt" area by our subjects that serious doubt exists whether this feature of the programming system is necessary. Similarly, there seemed to be little reason to use the testing mode of operation of the machine, and serious thought should be taken as to whether it is superfluous. On the other hand, there seemed to be very positive advantages in presenting the same material in both familiarization and learning modes; the system whereby this is accomplished (at present through the use of shutters and two separate tape cartridges) might be made more efficient and economical through the use of modified electromechanical features.

References

CARROLL, JOHN B. (1963a) A primer of programmed instruction in foreign language teaching, *Int. Rev. Applied Linguistics*, **1**, 115–141.

CARROLL, JOHN B. (1963b) Research on teaching foreign languages. Ch. 21, pp. 1060–1100, In N. L. Gage (ed.) *Handbook of Research on Teaching* (a project of the American Educational Research Association), Rand McNally and Co., Chicago.

CARROLL, JOHN B. (1963c) A model of school learning, *Teachers College Record*, **64**, 723–33.

CARROLL, JOHN B. and SAPON, STANLEY M. (1958–9) *Modern Language Aptitude Test: Manual*, The Psychological Corporation, New York.

HAYES, ALFRED S., et al., A new look at learning, In William F. Bottiglia (ed.) *Current Issues in Language Teaching: Reports of the Working Committees*, 1962 Northeast Conference on The Teaching of Foreign Languages, American Classical League Service Bureau, Miami University, Oxford, Ohio.

HOLTON, J. S., KING, P. E., MATHIEU, G. and POND, K. S. (1961) *Sound Language Teaching: The State of The Art Today*, University Publishers, New York.

KOPSTEIN, F. F. and CAVE, R. T. (July 1962) *Preliminary Cost Comparison of Technical Training by Conventional and Programmed Learning Methods*, Aerospace Medical Division, Report No. MRL-TDR-62-79, Wright-Patterson Air Force Base, Ohio.

MARTY, FERNAND (1962) *Programming a Basic Foreign Language Course: Prospects for Self-instruction*, Audio-visual Publications, Box 5497, Roanoke, Va.

MORTON, F. R. (1960) *The Language Laboratory as A Teaching Machine*, Series Pre-prints and Reprints, Vol. 1, Michigan Univ., Language Laboratory, Ann Arbor, Mich.

ROCKLYN, EUGENE H., MOREN, RICHARD I. and ZINOVIEFF, ANDRE (Jan. 1962) *Development and Evaluation of Training Methods for The Rapid Acquisition of Language Skills*, HumRRO Report No. 9, George Washington Univ. Human Resources Research Office, Washington, D.C.

SALTZMAN, IRVING J. (1963) Techniques used in the construction of a completely self-instructional, one semester, modern college course in Russian, In Francis W. Gravit and Albert Valdman (eds.) *Structural Drill and The Language Laboratory*, Indiana Univ., Bloomington, Ind. (Also published as Part III, *Int. J. Amer. Linguistics*, **29**, No. 2; Publication 27 of the Indiana Univ. Research Center in Anthropology, Folklore, and Linguistics.)

TEWKSBURY, M. GARDNER (1948) *Speak Chinese*, Yale University Press, New Haven, Conn.

WAITE, D. P. (1963) *Physical Requirements for Teaching Machines Using Graphic Displays,* Information Dynamics Corp., Wakefield, Mass. (Report to Northeastern Univ.; Supplement to Final Report for Grant No. 7-31-0570-161, U.S. Office of Education.)

WANG, FANG-YÜ (1953) *Read Chinese; Vol. I, A Beginning Text in The Chinese Character,* Pao-ch'en Lee (ed.), Institute of Far Eastern Languages, Yale Univ., New Haven, Conn.

CHAPTER III

A Study of Programmed Self-instruction for Seventh-grade Learners

GERALD NEWMARK

System Development Corporation, Santa Monica, California

ONE of the most serious obstacles to learning foreign languages in our schools is the lock-step system—the system by which all students progress as a group, from lesson to lesson, at a more or less fixed and predetermined pace, irrespective of the degree to which the students have mastered previous material.

It does not take much imagination to realize what would happen in an activity such as skiing if learners who had not yet learned how to walk, turn, and stop on skis were required to descend a mountain: many of them would break their legs. Yet in teaching students to understand, speak, read, and write a foreign language, our lock-step system probably has similar effects, although not as obvious or dramatic as a broken leg. These effects are expressed in student discouragement, failure, and discontinuance of language study after one or two years, or as soon as school requirements have been satisfied. Thus, many students who would be capable of acquiring a second language are not given a real opportunity to do so.

When the language laboratory first came on the scene, it was heralded as a revolutionary development which would do much to individualize and improve language instruction. In my view, the contribution of the language laboratory, to date, has been minimal. Most published reports on the language lab are highly favorable, but in visits to labs and in talks with students, teachers, and administrators, I have gained the impression that the professional literature presents a somewhat rose-colored picture and that much disenchantment with the lab exists. Many administrators view the language laboratory as nothing but a headache; many teachers use it only when required to do so; and many students are experiencing the same difficulties and frustrations as they did before its advent.

Data on the number of labs in use throughout the country is plentiful, but objective data concerning lab-students' achievement is indeed scarce. It is not hard to understand why negative information rarely gets into print. An administrator who has just spent $15,000 on a lab installation will find it difficult to write an article entitled, "How We Threw $15,000 Down the Drain".

The fact that the language lab may not have accomplished all that was hoped for should not be surprising or necessarily discouraging. For one thing, the language lab is not an educational method, technique, or system of instruction, but rather a set of hardware—a vehicle for presenting material—and, as such, it is no better than the material it uses and the system in which it is used.

I believe the language lab has considerable potential for improving language instruction. This potential has, as yet, not been realized in our schools because (1) appropriate materials have not been available, (2) it has been used largely in a group-mode system, with all students listening to the same material at the same time, and (3) even where students work alone, with individually selected exercises and lessons, the language course itself generally has been imbedded in a traditional lock-step organizational system.

The potential of the language lab, for both teaching and research, will be more fully realized with the development of materials that facilitate effective self-instruction. Programmed instruction offers considerable promise of providing such materials. A very positive interaction between programmed learning and the language lab appears to be in the offing. The language lab should serve as an excellent facility for research and development of programmed materials since it provides the equipment necessary for individual instruction; in turn, programmed materials should stimulate experimentation with new methods of teaching foreign languages and new patterns of organizing foreign language courses, which will make ever-increasing and more effective use of language laboratories. Programmed instruction also provides precise records of student responses which should contribute to our knowledge of the learning process and to the improvement of materials.

Before discussing a study in foreign language programming, conducted at System Development Corporation, it might be worthwhile to review briefly some of the principal characteristics of programmed learning. First, what is programmed learning? The term is often used synonymously with teaching machines, but this is misleading. Programmed learning actually refers to the material or the program, as it is called, that goes into the machine. This program can be presented not only by machine but also in book form, as a programmed text. In fact, over 90% of commercially available programs appear in programmed text format. The following are generally emphasized as the main characteristics of programmed instruction:

1. *Specification of objectives.* The terminal behavior, or the desired student response upon completion of the program, is clearly and precisely specified in full detail in advance.

2. *Gradual progression.* Material is organized into a series of small, carefully graded steps or items of instruction, gradually increasing in difficulty and complexity.

3. *Active participation.* Each item of instruction generally requires some specific response by the student (usually an overt response).

4. *Immediate reinforcement.* Each student response is reinforced by immediate knowledge of results (that is, knowledge of the correctness of the response).

5. *Successful performance.* Since each item in the program essentially prepares the student for the next one, the student makes few errors and practices mostly correct responses.

6. *Provision for individual differences.* Each student progresses through the program at his own rate of speed; in some programs, varying sequences are provided for students of varying abilities.

7. *Built-in system for improving the materials.* The programmer receives continuous feedback on the effectiveness of the material.

During the development of the program, items are tried out on a sample of the student population for whom they are intended. Whenever an error is made, the programmer asks himself what is wrong with the material, rather than what is wrong with the student. Ineffective items are revised or eliminated.

A Study to Develop More Flexible Programming Methods

Overview

For the past two years, in a study partly supported by the United States Office of Education, System Development Corporation has been studying programmed instruction in four subject matter areas—reading and arithmetic at the first-grade level, geometry at the high school level, and Spanish at the seventh-grade level. The emphasis in this study has been on exploring means of making programs more responsive to individual differences among learners and on developing rules and procedures for writing and improving programs. The study has also sought to determine what generalizations about programming could be applied across subject matter areas and age levels.

The following general procedures were used in all four subject matter areas. A linear program was administered to one student at a time. If he had difficulty in responding to any of the items in the program, he was interviewed immediately so that the cause of his difficulty could be determined. In an attempt to remedy the difficulty, the experimenter then tutored the student, using a variety of techniques. When the difficulty was resolved, the experimenter recorded the program sequence or techniques that seemed to be effective. The process of tutorial modifications continued until a sufficient number of changes warranted a major revision of the program. The revised program was then given to other students. Subsequent program revisions were made in the same manner. Formal experimental comparisons were made when there appeared to be a substantial difference between the latest revision and the original version of the program. If no significant difference was obtained, the revision process was continued. Empirical iterations were continued until differences were not only statistically significant, but also judged to be practically significant in favor of the revised program. The data which had been collected during the tutoring sessions and the student responses to the different versions of the program were then analyzed. The analysis resulted in generalizations concerning modifications that accounted for the improvement in the program.

This technique of using successive empirical iterations of intensive tutoring sessions to determine the branching structure and variations in the program differs markedly from current practice in program revision. More typically, remedial branches are inserted at reasonable junctures, and changes are made in the main stream of the program when there is evidence of excessive error rate; item changes are typically based on plausible notions of what *should* work, rather than on techniques which have actually been tried and *do* work. An account of the work conducted in Spanish, as part of this project, is presented below.

Description of Original Spanish Program

A programmed course in beginning Spanish, published by a commercial company, was selected for this study. It is designed for use by students without assistance of a teacher and attempts to teach simultaneously the four basic language skills; listening comprehension, speaking, reading, and writing. Unit one, the first 316 items of the program, was chosen as the starting point for the study. This unit covers a good sample of the basic Spanish sound system, a limited number of lexical items, and some important aspects of Spanish grammar (e.g., declarative, interrogative, and negative word order in the present tense, position of descriptive adjectives, possessive adjectives, definite and indefinite masculine articles). The program is linear; all students go through all the same items.

The materials consist of a programmed textbook containing instructions to the student, visual stimuli (pictures and writing), space for written responses, and written confirmation of written responses. The student has a mask to cover the correct answers until he has made his response. He then uncovers the mask to check his answer with the correct one. The texts are integrated with tape recordings containing auditory stimuli and auditory confirmation of oral responses.

Subjects

Subjects were provided by the Culver City Junior High School in the Culver City School District and by Lincoln Junior High School in the Santa Monica Unified School District. In all, 89 seventh-grade students took part in the study; 29 in individual tutorial sessions and 60 in three formal comparisons of the original and revised programs. Most of the students had no knowledge of Spanish. Some of the students had previously been exposed to a limited amount of Spanish in elementary school. However, a pretest indicated that they recalled only a few of the words and grammatical structures used in the program.

Physical Setting and Procedures

The study took place in SDC's CLASS (Computer-Based Laboratory for Automated School Systems) facility (see last section in this chapter for a description of CLASS). Sessions with individual students took place in the small counseling room. The experimental comparisons, involving twenty students simultaneously, took place in the larger instructional areas.

During the individual learning sessions, the student worked at a desk in a small, enclosed room which resembled a recording booth. A one-way glass enabled an observer, outside the room, to look in without being observed by the occupant. A microphone, hanging from the ceiling, was attached to a tape recorder outside the room, and all student oral responses were recorded. The student had the programmed text and a tape recorder on which to play the auditory portion of the program. All instruction took place at SDC and the student was told not to practice elsewhere.

The purpose of the experiment was explained to the student and use of the equipment and materials was demonstrated. A questionnaire was administered to ascertain the student's attitudes toward learning a second language. Upon completion of the program, criterion tests in listening comprehension, reading, writing, and speaking were administered.

The first few students went through the program without being tutored. The experimenter observed the student through the one-way glass, made item-specific notes in a copy of the programmed text and general remarks in a separate notebook, helped remedy problems with the equipment, clarified instructions upon request by the student, but gave no help with the Spanish content. When tutoring began, the experimenter remained in the room with the student, questioning him and helping him whenever he had difficulty.

Notes were kept on remedies tried and the results. When a particular remedy appeared effective, an attempt was made to incorporate it into subsequent sessions with the same student and with later students. Such revisions to the program were made as needed, on a day-to-day basis, by writing changes in the programmed text, by inserting new pages in the text, and by replacing portions of the tape-recorded auditory stimuli. When a number of changes made it desirable, complete sections of the text were revised and reproduced and a new master tape recorded. Revisions were based on (1) observations during the tutorial sessions, (2) analysis of written responses in the programmed text, (3) analysis of diagnostic test results, and (4) analysis of the post-training criterion test results.

Criterion Tests

The program content was analyzed to determine the emphasis given to each of the four basic language skills. Based on this analysis, a post-training criterion test was constructed covering each of the four skills. In the scoring, listening comprehension and speaking received the most weight, followed by reading, and then writing.

In the test on listening comprehension, each item consisted of a tape-recorded Spanish stimulus and five printed English responses, from which the student selected the one most closely approximating the stimulus. In reading, the student read a Spanish sentence and selected from among five printed English alternatives the one most closely corresponding to the Spanish stimulus. In writing, the student had to rewrite Spanish sentences making certain transformations (e.g., change affirmative statements to the negative), write Spanish answers to questions about pictures, and complete Spanish sentences when given the English equivalent of missing portions.

The speaking test is modeled after Pimsleur's *A French Speaking Proficiency Test** and consists of four parts: vocabulary recall, pronunciation, grammatical usage, and fluency. Objectivity in scoring is increased, since for each part of the test only one aspect of speaking performance is evaluated. Parts I and III are designed so that the items are either right or wrong. In Parts II and IV, rating scales are used. In our study, students' responses were recorded and then judged by three native-speaking Spanish teachers. These judges were trained on the scoring procedures, using the tests of students who had completed the program during the intitial revision phase. After satisfactory interjudge reliability had been achieved, the judges evaluated the speaking tests from the final experimental comparison. The mean scores of the three evaluations were used in the final comparison. The interjudge reliability for the final comparison was as follows: for the original program group (coefficient of concordance $= 0 \cdot 97$, $p < 0 \cdot 01$); for the revised program group (coefficient of concordance $= 0 \cdot 84$, $p < 0 \cdot 01$).

Initial Tryout of Original Program

A tryout of the original program with the first eight subjects resulted in a mean achievement of 69% on all tests combined. The mean achievement for the subtests was as follows: listening comprehension, 74%; reading, 90%; writing, 59%; and speaking, 59%. Considerable range in achievement was evident (i.e., total all

* Pimsleur, Paul, A French speaking proficiency test, *French Review*, **34,** 470–9, April 1961.

tests, 33–86%; listening, 28–100%; writing, 31–85%; reading, 69–100%; and speaking, 15–87%). The mean time to complete the program was 252 minutes (4 hours 12 minutes) and the range was 185–365 minutes (3 hours 5 minutes–6 hours 5 minutes).

The results indicated that for these eight students the goal of programmed learning (i.e., having all students master almost all of the material, differing only in the time to complete the program) was not realized, and that therefore the program was open to further improvement.

Initial Revisions

Individual learning sessions with the first twenty-three pupils resulted in the following principal changes to the program:

1. *Elimination of unnecessary and irrelevant items.* The first forty-one items in the program provide the student with practice on individual vowel sounds. The student is supposed to learn first to discriminate, and then to reproduce, correct Spanish sounds. The principal technique used is that of contrasting incorrect English sounds with correct Spanish sounds (i.e., the English and Spanish pronunciations of the same vowel sounds are given).

Since most students were able to make these discriminations after a few trials, subsequent items of this type seemed superfluous. Furthermore, when students were presented with the incorrect and correct models and asked to reproduce orally the correct Spanish sounds, they frequently repeated the English or both the English and Spanish sounds. Consequently, these items were eliminated from the program.

The program introduced new Spanish words by dividing them into syllables for initial practice on each syllable. As with the vowels, the Spanish syllable was contrasted with an English syllable. Again, as with the vowels, students frequently pronounced the incorrect English syllables or both the English and Spanish. Furthermore, when asked to pronounce the word as a whole, some students continued to pronounce each syllable separately. Consequently, all English–Spanish contrastive items were eliminated, thus exposing students only to correct Spanish models. Also, new words were introduced as a unit rather than by syllables.

2. *Providing additional practice in hearing prior to speaking.* Students frequently had difficulty in pronouncing new words and expressions accurately. In the original program, when a new word or phrase was introduced, the student would hear it once and immediately imitate it. The student would then hear the word a second time and repeat it again. This procedure was revised so that new material would be presented three times before the student spoke it. The student would then repeat three times after the Spanish model.

3. *Providing additional practice on difficult structures.* The original program contained many important features of Spanish structure. However, the steps in the program were apparently too big for many of the students to master. Many of the difficulties one would anticipate for an American learning Spanish occurred; e.g., incorrect position of *no* in negative sentences, improper word order of descriptive adjectives, the use of two negatives in the same sentence, etc. More items were added to the program in order to provide practice on those aspects of Spanish grammar causing the most trouble. Generally, there was a much slower build-up in task complexity, especially in writing in Spanish, consistently the weakest area according to criterion test scores.

4. *Difficulty in following instructions.* Students consistently had difficulty in following program instructions. The major problem appeared to be excessive variability in required response behavior. Each item required a different type of response and, consequently, a new set of instructions in English which students had to read carefully but often did not. Some examples of student errors are (1) repeating after the model when asked just to listen; (2) listening when asked to repeat; (3) writing a response when asked to say it and vice-versa; (4) making a response in English instead of Spanish; (5) not stopping the tape at the appropriate time.

Several steps were taken to remedy the difficulties: (1) Instructions "listen" or "repeat" were added to the tape just prior to the stimulus or confirmation material. (2) The written English instructions in the text were simplified and shortened and key words were underlined (e.g., <u>say aloud, write in Spanish</u>). (3) English reading was reduced by replacing instructions with symbols (e.g., "check your answer with the tape" was replaced by a check mark "√"). (4) The sound of a horn was used on the tape as a signal to stop the tape recorder; later, preprogrammed automatic stops replaced the horn (see description of sound system in CLASS, in section at end of this chapter).

5. *Addition of frequent diagnostic tests.* In spite of a low error rate on the program itself, some students made low scores on the criterion test. This indicated a need for more frequent testing in order to determine whether the student was actually mastering the material as he went along.

Short diagnostic tests were prepared for each of the four basic language skills covering fifty-item segments of the program. They were administered at fifty-item intervals, and tutoring took place at this time rather than every time the student made an error. The practice of tutoring the student every time he made an error had several shortcomings. It caused frequent interruptions which seemed to interfere with students' concentration. When left untutored, students frequently corrected themselves on subsequent items. Also, it was easier to discern the pattern of student difficulties by observing several errors over a series of items.

First Experimental Comparison

Although the original program was designed primarily for individual independent study, the publishers indicate that it can be used in a group mode. In this mode, all students progress from item to item simultaneously. The students signal the teacher when they have read the instructions in their programmed text. The teacher then plays the tape to present the auditory stimulus and waits until all students have completed their responses before playing the confirmation message.

The first comparison of the original program with the revised program was in the group mode. Twenty seventh-grade students from Culver City Junior High School were randomly assigned to each of two groups, one to use the original program, the other to use the revised program. The two groups did not differ significantly on the total combined score or on any of the individual tests (i.e., listening, reading, writing, and speaking).

Several shortcomings were observed in the group mode with both versions of the program. Since the pace was geared to the slowest student in the class, students became restless and talkative while waiting for others to finish reading instructions or to complete a response. With oral responses, the most aggressive student would speak up first and other students would imitate him (whether he was correct or incorrect). The noise level was generally high and the students at times acted silly. In contrast to this, in the individual mode, the students exhibited a high degree of concentration and seriousness.

Subsequent Revisions and Second Experimental Comparison

Results of the first experimental comparison indicated a wide range of achievement among the students on the total test scores as well as on the individual tests in listening comprehension, speaking, reading, and writing. Individual differences in student ability to handle particular language skills were great. To provide more individualized practice, a limited form of branching was initiated. The revised program was divided into five units of approximately fifty items each. A combined diagnostic and review exercise was provided for each of the four skills, at the end of each unit, so that a student could receive additional practice with any particular skill before proceeding to the next unit. Content of the review emphasized those language elements which caused the most trouble in the program.

A second formal comparison of the initial and the revised program was conducted. Twenty seventh-grade students were randomly assigned to two groups. The comparison was conducted in the individual mode. Each student worked independently, at his own rate of speed, and upon completion of the program was administered an individual test in listening comprehension, reading, writing, and speaking. The mean scores on each individual test, as well as on the combined test, did not differ significantly.

Development of the Final Program Version

Subsequent tutorial sessions were devoted to improving the branching procedures and the remedial exercises. The results thus far had indicated that the program was still too difficult for some students, while others mastered most of the material. Revision of the program to provide smaller steps and additional practice would penalize higher-achieving students. Adding remedial branches for the benefit of the slower students would cause them to experience frequent failure before undertaking the necessary remedial practice. Therefore, it was decided to provide separate tracks for slow and fast students. These tracks were parallel in content and format but differed in such dimensions as step size, amount and type of practice, cueing, and sequencing of subskills. Track A was the fast track; Track B the slow. The same end-of-unit diagnostic tests (one for each of the four basic skills) were used for both tracks. Branching took place at the end of each unit on the basis of the diagnostic test results. Branching was done by individual language skill so that a student who had trouble with one skill undertook remedial exercises in that skill only.

The revised program was tried out individually with six students to evaluate the effectiveness of the branching. After administering the program to each student, further revisions were made, especially to the remedial exercises. Also, a second level of branching was added to the program. Thus, at the end of each unit, two levels of branching were provided for each of the four basic skills. The first level was a fast branch providing some additional practice for students making minor or careless errors. The second level was a slow branch for students having serious difficulty with particular linguistic problems. It provided extensive remedial practice.

When a student made low scores on all four diagnostic tests at the end of the unit, he was sometimes required to repeat the unit. This procedure was not effective in improving performance. The student generally repeated the same mistakes. Repetition of a unit was not used as a remedial branch until the student had shown improvement based on remedial exercises. At this point repetition seemed to provide valuable overlearning.

All students began with Unit I of the fast track (Track A). The results of the diagnostic tests administered to each student at the end of Unit I showed a wide range of achievement, and subsequent branching paths followed by these students differed considerably. The time required to complete the program varied from 166 to 766 minutes (2 hours 46 minutes to 12 hours 46 minutes). The mean total scores on the criterion tests, when compared with the results of the previous experimental comparisons, showed an increase in achievement over all previous revisions and over the original program.

Fig. 4 is a flow diagram depicting the branching structure used in the final program version. Activities are represented by rectangles, and the direction of flow between activities is shown by arrows. Decision points or branches are represented by diamond-shaped figures. The alternative branches or routes are represented by arrows originating from the points of the diamond.

The flow through the program is as follows:

1. *All students begin with Unit I, Track A (fast track).*

2. *All students complete Unit I.*

3. *All students take diagnostic tests in the four skills,* i.e., listening comprehension, speaking, reading, and writing. Three alternative branches are possible at this point *(a, b,* and *c).* If the student makes satisfactory scores on all tests, he takes Branch *a* and goes on to Unit II in Track A. If the student has made a limited number of minor or careless errors in any of the skills, he takes Branch *b,* which provides first-level remedial exercises in any or all of the four skills. In each skill where the student has made an excessive number of errors, he takes Branch *c,* which provides second-level remedial exercises in any or all of the skills. The student may be branched to *b* for some skills and to *c* for others at this point. (Branching decisions were made by the experimenter.)

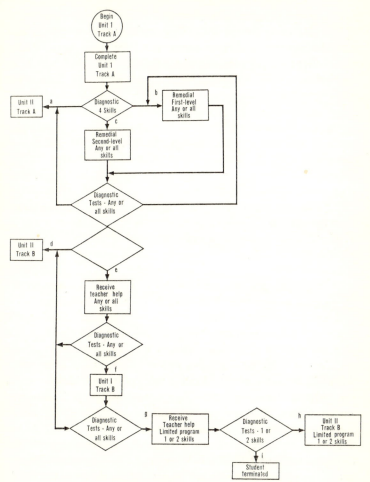

FIG. 4. Branching structure in final program version.

4. *Diagnostic tests are readministered for each skill in which the student has taken remedial exercises.* Four branches are available at this point. If the student has had a minimum amount of remedial work and his scores are satisfactory, he will take Branch *a* and go on to Unit II, Track A. If he has had more extensive remedial work

and his scores are now satisfactory he will take Branch *d* and go on to Unit II, Track B. For those skills in which the student is still making a limited number of minor errors, he takes Branch *b* and goes to first-level remedial exercises. For those skills in which he is still having serious problems, he is branched to the teacher for help (Branch e).

5. *Diagnostic tests are readministered for those skills in which the student has received additional help.* Two alternative routes are available. In Branch *d*, the student who has improved sufficiently goes on to Unit II, Track B (slow track). If the student has not improved sufficiently to go on to Unit II, Track B, he takes Branch *f* (i.e., Unit I, Track B).

6. *Following Unit I, Track B, diagnostic tests are readministered.* Two branches are possible. In *d*, the student goes on to Unit II, Track B. In *g*, the student is again branched to the teacher for help but this time in a limited program in which instruction is limited to one or two skills.

7. *Diagnostic tests are readministered in skills in which the student has received teacher help.* Two branches are then available. If the student's achievement is satisfactory, he will continue on to Unit II, Track B, limited program (Branch *h*). (He will stay in the limited program until he achieves satisfactory scores on the final criterion test. At that point, he may again undertake instruction in the other skills.) In Branch *i*, if it is decided that further instruction, under the learning conditions provided, would not be profitable, the student is terminated from the program.

8. *The student may be branched from Track A to Track B and vice-versa during the program.* The results of the student's performance on Unit I of Track A seemed to be a reliable screening device for determining whether the student would be in the fast or slow track, since students branched to Track B usually stayed there throughout the program.

Final Experiment Comparison

Upon completion of the final version of the revised program, an experimental comparison was made between it and the original program in SDC's CLASS (Computer Based Laboratory for Automated School Systems) facility. Twenty seventh-grade students from Lincoln Junior High School in the Santa Monica Unified School District participated in the experiment. Ten pairs of students were matched on the basis of IQ, grade-point average in English, Social Studies and Math. One student from each pair was randomly assigned to Group 1 (revised program) while the other student was then placed in Group 2 (original program).

The mean scores on the total of all tests, as well as on each individual test, were higher for the revised program group. These differences are significant for the total of all tests ($t = 3\cdot19$, $p < 0\cdot01$); for listening ($t = 2\cdot07$, $p < 0\cdot05$); for reading ($t = 2\cdot64$, $p < 0\cdot01$); for writing ($t = 4\cdot17$, $p < 0\cdot01$); and for speaking ($t = 2\cdot81$, $p < 0\cdot01$). A one-tailed t-test was used because we predicted the direction of the results in favor of the revised program. The variability for the revised program group was considerably reduced both for the total score and the individual tests. However, except for the reading test the variability was sufficient to suggest the need for further improvement of the two main tracks as well as the possibility of a third track. In fact, a third, faster track was developed but was not tested.

For this comparison, the mean time to complete the revised program was higher (4 hours 23 minutes) than for the original program (3 hours). The range for the revised program (2 hours 14 minutes–6 hours 34 minutes) was also greater than that for the original program (2 hours–4 hours 4 minutes). It would appear that in a flexible program using extensive branching procedures, the amount of extra time needed by slower students to achieve satisfactory results is much greater than the amount of time saved by faster students.

Conclusions

The research described in this report was exploratory. The purpose was to discover how a system of instruction could be improved and to develop hypotheses concerning programming methods. A significant improvement was achieved through the technique of individual tutoring and iterative revisions. In the process, observations were made which permit some tentative conclusions.

1. *Programs can and should be made more responsive to individual differences in learners.* Linear programs are said to be effective when 90% or more of the students achieve 90% or more on the posttraining criterion test. In such a program, the steps generally have been made small enough so that the slower students achieve success. There is a question as to whether a considerable amount of the brighter students' time is being wasted. Boredom and frustration may also be problems with the more capable students.

The initial tryout of the original commercial program indicated that it was too difficult for many students, although a few mastered most of the material. Revising the program to provide smaller steps would have penalized the higher-achieving students. Adding remedial branches for the benefit of the slower students would not have been satisfactory, as it would have caused them to experience frequent failure before undertaking the necessary remedial practice. We found that separate tracks were necessary for slow and fast students. These tracks were parallel in content and format but differed in such dimensions as step size, amount and type of practice, cueing, and sequencing of subskills. Depending on the number of students having similar success or difficulty with the material, two or more tracks might be required in order to provide maximum responsiveness to individual differences.

Use of minimal steps in the initial development of a program obscures unnecessary and irrelevant items. If the initial tryout indicates high achievement for most students, the programmer does not know if the same results could have been accomplished with larger steps and in less time. The goal should be optimal steps rather than minimal steps. It would appear easier to get to optimal step size by starting with large steps rather than small ones. Excessively large steps are discovered immediately in initial tryouts. If an initial tryout indicates that the program is too difficult for most students, but that some students have mastered most of the material (as was the case in the tryout of the original program), then the original version might be considered as the basis for a fast track.

Branching is an important method of increasing a program's responsiveness to individual differences. Within the two-track program there were still considerable differences in student performance. Students' difficulties varied not only with individual linguistic elements but also with particular language skills. Failure to master material at each step of the way caused greater and greater difficulties as the program progressed and resulted in low performance on criterion tests. Remedial exercises leading to mastery were necessary; however, exercises which require practice in all skills waste time for some students. Branching was therefore introduced by language skill and by linguistic problem within each skill; thus, a student having difficulty with writing but not with the other three skills was able to receive additional help in writing alone.

Learning the four basic language skills simultaneously was very difficult for some students. For example, some students could not write English well; in learning a foreign language, it was unrealistic to expect them to do well in writing and at the same time in understanding, speaking, and reading. It seemed apparent that some of the students could have achieved satisfactory results if relieved of the necessity to learn all of them. Students who were having difficulty with all skills were branched to remedial exercises in one or two skills only. After satisfactory completion of all units, limited to one or two skills, the pupil went through the program again, concentrating this time on the remaining skills.

Ideally, when a language program has the objective of teaching the four basic language skills (listening, speaking, reading, and writing) it should be designed to enable pupils to receive training in one particular skill at a time or some combination of skills. Where satisfactory acquisition of all four skills seems unattainable or impracticable under the particular learning conditions, it should be possible to limit the terminal behavior to one or more skills without having to receive training in all of them.

2. *The teacher has an important role to play in connection with the use of programmed materials.* In the beginning of the study, the teacher was used to tutor students for the purpose of revising and

improving the materials. It was not until the development of the final version that the teacher was actually used as a branch in the program.

At the seventh-grade level, it appeared that relatively few students were capable enough or motivated enough for completely independent study. Monitoring, testing, branching, and remedial tutoring were important functions of the teacher.

In the early stages of the program, the important function of the teacher was to see that the students were performing according to directions. Slower students had intermittent problems in following directions throughout the program, especially when new material or new tasks were introduced. The teacher monitored the students very closely during the early stages; later, when slower and faster students had been identified, the teacher spent more time monitoring the slow students.

Self-scoring of end-of-unit diagnostic tests and self-branching to remedial units by students were not effective. Students were generally careless in scoring. They were also reluctant to branch themselves to remedial units since they wanted to keep up with their friends. When the teacher scored the tests and branched the students, learning improved.

When a student's achievement failed to improve significantly after going through the remedial exercises, he was referred to the teacher for help. The teacher was able to provide a variety of exercises and techniques which would have been impractical to include in the program itself. Further, the teacher provided a type of personal encouragement (e.g., a smile, a remark, etc.) which was not possible when the student worked on the program by himself. Student restlessness decreased and concentration increased during and after contact with the teacher. When several students finished a unit simultaneously or needed help at the same time, an overload situation occurred. This was relieved, in part, by reducing the frequency of the diagnostic testing for the higher-achieving students. However, waiting did occur. This problem, as well as the entire question of the role of the teacher and teacher–pupil ratio in a partially self-instructional system, needs study.

3. *Excessive variability in required response behavior from item to item can interfere with learning.* In the original program, each item required a new set of instructions which students had to read carefully but did not. It would appear that at this age level, and especially for the average and slow students, response behavior should be kept constant over a series of items so that one set of instructions is sufficient for all items in the series. This was done in the revised version, primarily with the remedial exercises. Variety can be introduced in other ways; for example, in the stimulus materials, in the feedback materials, and with each new series of items.

4. *With programmed instruction, self-evaluation by students may be a problem not only in pronunciation but also in other aspects of speaking.* Students did not pay sufficient attention to confirmation messages on the tape and, consequently, often proceeded to the next item thinking a response was correct when, in fact, it had been wrong. We first required students to evaluate each response overtly by making a mark in the programmed text. In addition to forcing the student to focus more closely on the confirmation message, we thought the scoring procedure would increase motivation. This approach was not successful. Students would frequently forget to evaluate or evaluate incorrectly. Incorrect evaluation would occur even in the case of structural items where discrepancies between the student's response and the confirmation message should have been obvious. This phenomenon should be studied further since most foreign language programmers have been primarily concerned with the student's ability to evaluate his own pronunciation.

In the final program version, instructions were changed so that pupils not only listened to confirmation messages but also repeated them. This insured that the student would at least say the correct response before proceeding to the next item.

5. *For most seventh-grade students working with programmed instruction, short, frequent instructional sessions are better than longer ones.* Students become restless after 15 or 20 minutes of working by themselves; 45-minute sessions are too long for most students.

(In this case it may have been partially due to the fact that instructional sessions were held after a full day of regular school.)

6. *Frequent diagnostic testing improves learning.* In spite of low error rate on the program itself, some students made low scores on criterion tests. The diagnostic tests provided a means of determining whether the student actually was mastering the material as he went along. They helped pinpoint student difficulties and served as the basis for assigning remedial work. Also, they increased motivation by providing short-range goals and frequent indications of progress.

7. *Programs designed primarily for individual self-instruction are not readily adaptable to group instruction.* The Spanish program in our study was designed primarily for individual instruction. When it was used in a group mode, certain shortcomings became evident. One was the large amount of English instruction for each item, which produced restlessness in students waiting for others to finish reading or making a response. Another problem was that students often imitated the first responder even when the response was incorrect. However, these may be shortcomings of this particular program and a program designed for both group and individual instruction could be successful (for example, a program that taught listening comprehension separately would be more readily adaptable to group instruction).

8. *Special training in discriminating between Spanish and English sounds does not enhance student performance.* The extent to which a student can evaluate his own oral responses is an important consideration for language programmers. Some programmers have assumed that the student must first receive specific training in aural discrimination in order to become an effective evaluator of his own pronunciation. Depending on the programmer, discrimination training generally has meant distinguishing between good and poor pronunciation or English and native pronunciation, or distinguishing between similar sounds within the total phonology of the foreign language.

Every person who understands and speaks a language has learned how to discriminate among the sounds of that language. In foreign language instruction, however, a major question is whether this ability to discriminate must be taught explicitly or whether it is a by-product of some other type of training or experience.

The discrimination training used in the original program, that of contrasting correct Spanish sounds with incorrect English sounds, was not effective. Elimination of these items saved time and appeared to have no adverse effect on achievement. Controlled experimentation is needed to determine whether or not this and other types of discrimination training do, in fact, improve learning.

9. *Students generally react favorably to programmed materials.* Pretraining questionnaires indicated that most of the students were interested in learning a foreign language but not very confident in their ability to do so. Most felt that learning a foreign language would be difficult. Posttraining questionnaires indicated that most students liked this way of learning and felt that it was easy. (Even those who did most poorly in achievement felt that the learning was easy.) Some students did express a preference for studying with a teacher in a group situation.

Some typical student responses to questions follow:

Q. What did you like most about your Spanish lessons?

"I found it very easy to learn the material."

"Being able to find my mistakes when I make them and being able to correct them (in my mind) right away."

"The fact that I could go along at my own speed."

"I learned something fast enough so it wasn't dull."

Q. What did you like least?

"Sometimes I felt that I was going too slowly."

"Some of the directions didn't seem clear; but it was probably my own fault because after the meaning was pointed out they became very clear."

"I got tired when I was in there for too long a time. Getting up and walking for a few minutes every 15 minutes or so made me feel better."

"They didn't cover very well some of the questions which were on the tape."

"The same procedure was used a little too much."

Q. What caused you the most difficulty?

"Remembering the order of words in sentences."

"Repeating long sentences. Placement of the adjective."

"Negative forms of sentences and asking questions out loud in Spanish when given the English question in writing."

"Copying what I heard on the tape."

"Sentence structure. Where to place adjectives."

"Saying phrases in Spanish."

10. *Self-study by seventh-grade students using programmed materials can be effective.* In spite of apparent weaknesses in the original program when used at the seventh-grade level, some students achieved high scores on the criterion tests and apparently had the ability and motivation to work independently. This alone would be significant, even if programs could not be written which proved effective with larger numbers of students at this age level. Qualified language teachers could spend more time with students of lower aptitude. It also would permit students to study languages which otherwise would not be available in the school curriculum.

It is also important to note that some students, who probably would have been failures or dropouts in a group-mode, lock-step situation, were able to achieve a substantial amount of learning with the highly flexible revised program.

On the other hand, most of the students seemed to lack the ability and motivation for completely independent study. Judging by the restlessness of students after short periods of working alone and their inability to sustain concentration, it appears that motivation would be a serious problem in any extended program of individual self-instruction. With better and more interesting materials this problem could be reduced; however, with students of this age level, some combination of individual, small-group, and large-group study would seem necessary, as well as teacher presence

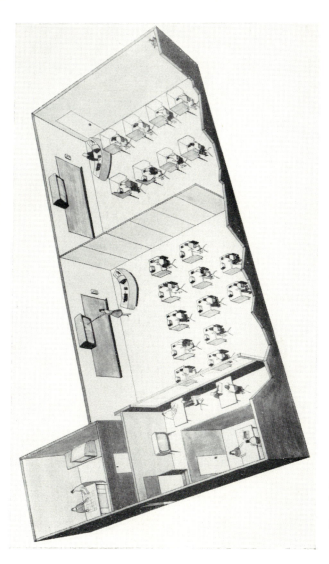

FIG. 5. Perspective drawing showing overview of Computer-Based Laboratory for Automated School Systems (CLASS). Two classrooms at right permit mixed modes of instruction. A counseling area and an observation deck are shown at lower left and an administrative office is represented at upper left. All areas have access to the data-processing capabilities of a Philco 2000 computer (not shown).

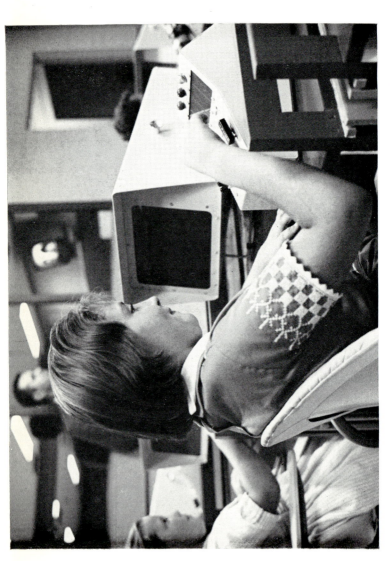

FIG. 6. Student receiving individualized automated instruction in CLASS. A viewing device is shown at the student's left and a response device at her right.

FIG. 7. Students receiving group automated instruction in CLASS. The instructional materials are displayed over the television monitor at upper right; students respond individually and receive individual feedback through separate response devices. Mr. Newmark is in the background.

Fig. 8. Teacher's console in CLASS. The display panel at left alerts the teacher to student learning problems. Push-buttons on units at left allow the teacher to call up computer-generated displays on individual students, or on the class as a whole, through cathode-ray tube at right.

A Computer-Based Laboratory for Automated School Systems

General Description of CLASS Facility

In 1961, System Development Corporation constructed an experimental Computer-Based Laboratory for Automated School Systems (CLASS). CLASS permits research on the use of modern data-processing equipment, not only for instruction but for other important educational activities such as counseling, class assignment scheduling, and the storage and processing of student and fiscal records.

Figure 5 shows an overview of the CLASS facility. Flexible control capabilities, storage and retrieval capacity, and other data-processing functions are provided in CLASS by a large digital computer, the Philco 2000. (This computer is located in another area and is consequently not illustrated in the drawing.) Various display and response devices in CLASS are connected by cables to the computer.

The largest area of CLASS, shown at the right of Fig. 5, is an instructional area that can be divided into two separate classrooms by a sound-attenuating partition. Up to twenty students can be given concurrent automated instruction, with each student receiving a different sequence of materials and proceeding at his own pace. (This capacity is determined by the classroom space and input/output channels available in the experimental facility; the Philco computer could be used to provide concurrent independent instruction for several hundred students.) Or, if desired, any number of the twenty students can receive group instruction through television or film projection, conventional lecture, or textbook. CLASS is designed to permit research on the effectiveness of different combinations of instructional techniques for different educational requirements.

Figure 6 shows students receiving programmed instruction in

the classroom area. Individualized automated instruction in CLASS utilizes students' display and response devices. Instructional items are stored on a film strip that can be projected on the screen of a student's individual viewing device (shown at the student's left). The student moves from one instructional frame to another by turning a crank on the side of the viewer.

A separate control box (at the student's right) contains computer-controlled digital counters that show the student the number of the frame he should view at any point during the lesson. The sequence of frame numbers displayed to the student is determined by the lesson control program and by student responses inserted through multiple-choice buttons on the individual control box. After each response, the student receives feedback in the form of colored lights indicating whether he has answered correctly, and telling him the proper response alternative. A bright student may be allowed to skip many remedial frames in going from one topic to another, while a slower student may be directed to a longer sequence appropriate to his particular learning needs.

A group mode of programmed instruction is also possible in CLASS. In this mode all students view the same instructional frames through a television monitor or other group display (Fig. 7). Each student responds individually through his control box and receives individualized feedback about his performance.

In group programmed instruction the sequence and pace must be adjusted to the needs of the entire group. This necessarily means a loss in responsiveness to individual student differences, but the group mode may still be quite effective for relatively homogeneous groups and in educational situations where students are encouraged to cooperate in reaching group solutions. Furthermore, the group mode permits concurrent instruction of many more students, for a given computer, than is possible in the individual mode.

A special console in each of the classroom areas (Fig. 8) permits supervision and monitoring of student performance by a teacher or experimenter. When a student makes too many response errors or otherwise fails to meet preprogrammed performance criteria, the

Fig. 9. Counseling office in CLASS. While interviewing students, the counselor can call up computer-generated displays giving summaries of student grades, attendance, and other background data.

computer causes a light to flash at the teacher's console indicating which student is having difficulty. The teacher can then call up several types of computer-generated displays on a cathode-ray tube. One display indicates what topic the student is currently working on, how many errors he has made on that topic, and how many errors he has made on the entire lesson. Another display gives information about the student's previous course grades, attendance records, and other relevant background data. The teacher can also follow an individual student's item-by-item progress, noting what answers the student is giving to each item and what feedback he is receiving. This can all be accomplished by the teacher without leaving his own desk or disturbing the student. On the basis of such displays, the teacher can decide whether to let the erring student continue his programmed instruction, or to assign him to special remedial work in the form of textbooks, films, or private tutoring.

Computer-generated displays are also available at the teacher's console in the group mode of automated instruction. These displays provide summary information to the teacher about student responses to questions in the program, so that the teacher can control the program sequence and can interject remedial materials wherever necessary to clarify points of student misunderstanding.

At the lower left in Fig. 5 is an observation deck and counseling area. The counselor's office (Fig. 9) contains a display system and a control box. As the counselor interviews students, he can call up computer-generated displays giving background information about the student's aptitude, grade history, and class attendance record. Such displays may help the counselor to work more closely with teachers in diagnosing and alleviating student learning problems and in planning curricula that will be appropriate to the student's needs and abilities.

A further aid to the counselor is the computer-controlled class assignment schedule program, several versions of which are now under development in various parts of the country. This program can relieve the counselor of most of the routine clerical work involved in assigning students to classes, thereby freeing him for more individual counseling.

At the upper left in Fig. 5 is an administrative office where the operations of educational administrators may be analyzed and evaluated. Again, the computer can be of great assistance. It can store, analyze, and retrieve salary and logistical data for use by the administrator. It can summarize and print out records of students' background data and class attendance. It can analyze enrollment trends and provide statistical projections of these trends for use by the administrator in predicting future needs for plant construction, teacher hiring, curriculum modifications, and bus scheduling.

Sound System in CLASS

CLASS contains an electronic communication system typical of level-three language laboratories. The installation permits the distribution of recordings to students under the control of the instructor, and provides the opportunity for individual self-study at each student position. The intercommunication facilities of the system enable the teacher to monitor student activities, to talk with individuals or groups of students, and to have students talk with each other.

Each student position has an individual tape recorder, located in a drawer beneath the desk. The controls for operating the recorder are on the desk. With younger pupils it is possible to preload the tape and close the drawer so that they have access only to the controls.

Each tape recorder has four channels. Channel 1 contains the master program. Channel 2 records the master and the student response (when this is desired). Channel 3 provides an automatic stop system controlled by a tone burst on the tape. It is therefore possible to have the recorder stop automatically immediately after presentation of the stimulus material. The student then can take as much time as he needs to make his response. It also eliminates the student action of stopping the recorder, and any interference which might be caused by this action intervening between the stimulus and the response.

Provision is made for deactivating the automatic stop control when it is not desired. In addition to the hand control, a detachable foot switch is provided for restarting the tape mechanism after each automatic stop, and stopping it when it is in normal operation.

The system is so designed that a random-access tape-location capability can be added with a minimum of modification. Channel 4 would be used for this purpose. This capability would enable the student to go from any location on the tape to any other location quickly and accurately by a simple switch insertion. With more extensive branching procedures, the importance of such a system increases.

Future plans call for placing the random-access capability under computer as well as human control. The sound system will also eventually be synchronized with visual presentations emanating from the individual student viewer or from the TV.

CHAPTER IV

Toward Self-instruction in Foreign Language Learning*

ALBERT VALDMAN

University of Indiana

THE remarkable revolution in foreign language teaching methodology and technology, now labeled the "New Key", constitutes both the strength and the weakness of language teaching in the United States. While no efficient teaching of language as sound first and letters second is possible without the New Key type of materials which are becoming more plentiful with each succeeding year, and the wonderful gadgetry which is mushrooming across the land,† concentration on the inanimate and external components of foreign language instruction has diverted attention from its more fundamental components: time, the role of the teacher, the nature of the foreign language process, the structure of the teaching environment, and—oh, yes—the *student*. In this article I should like to show how these generally neglected components of foreign language instruction can best be interrelated and manipulated to make the design of foreign

---

* The research reported herein was performed pursuant to a Title VI research contract with the U.S. Office of Education, Department of Health, Education, and Welfare.

† It was unofficially reported that in 1961 about 2500 secondary schools and about 700 colleges and universities possessed some sort of language laboratory; the estimate as of October 1, 1962, was 5000 secondary schools and 800 institutions of higher learning.

language teaching systems more effective, efficient, and congruent with the learning theories and the technology currently being developed and applied.

The New Key is the direct heir of the Intensive Language Program of the early 1940's, which was inspired and manned by linguists, most of whom—including Leonard Bloomfield, whose *Outline Guide for the Practical Study of Foreign Languages* (1942), formulated the theories and precepts on which the New Key rests—had described and analyzed preliterate American Indian languages (Moulton, 1962). Because of his contact with languages for which no writing system existed, the linguist readily accepted that in language sound is primary and writing only a secondary derivative, or put more emphatically: "Language is the noises we make with our face and not the scratches we make with our fist." (Hall, 1950, p. 50.) The linguist viewed language as a complex aggregate of sensory and motor habits and concluded that nothing short of relentless repetition would lead to the audio-lingual fluency which contractual agencies such as the U.S. Army or the Department of State required of language trainees. Since even native speakers of a language are unable to describe these habits, most of which lie beyond their threshold of awareness, little profit is derived from the memorization and explication of rules; as Bloomfield put it, "Language learning is overlearning. Anything else is of no use." (Bloomfield, 1942, p. 12.)

Unlike the direct method enthusiast, the linguist did not throw out the baby with the bath water and *grammar* was very much—perhaps too much—in evidence in the foreign language courses he directed or the teaching materials whose preparation he supervised. Of course, to him *grammar* consisted of neither the memorization of rules nor the recitation of paradigms, nor was he concerned with linguistic etiquette or indeed with "predictors" of linguistic behavior; "grammatical rules were merely the description of the student's own performance . . . *summaries of behavior*" (Politzer and Staubach, 1961, p. 8). In New Key materials, grammar is presented inductively through *pattern drills* and statements about the grammatical features manifested in a set of drills are postponed until the student demonstrates fluency in the use of these features.

The Intensive Program's orientation of foreign language instruction toward the audio-lingual and its emphasis on massive contact resulted primarily from external circumstances, namely, the contracting agencies' very practical needs, and the use of common sense, which Descartes assures us is "la chose du monde la mieux partagée". The linguist's most important contributions *qua* linguist were the preparation of detailed descriptions of a variety of *spoken* languages, including the heretofore commonly taught languages (French, German, Spanish) and the general practice of contrasting the structure of the native and target languages to predict in advance probable points of difficulty and interference.

After two decades of experience, we can now attempt a fair evaluation of the pedagogical effectiveness and efficiency of the New Key. By definition, linguists are concerned with the structure of language and their attempt to deal with the processes that take place in the language classroom, be it in the very special conditions of the Foreign Service Institute or in an elementary school class, can be expected to fall quite short of the mark; for in foreign language instruction, the linguist's competence ends before practical problems of presentation and ordering of material and the organization of the instructional context are reached. Thus, obsessed with structure, the linguist never pondered over the process that takes place in the foreign language classroom, language *learning;* seldom did he construct controlled experiments to test some of the assertions he made *qua* language teacher, and he never suspected that the success of intensive-type instruction might be due to external factors—student motivation, intensive contact, and the like—rather than his operational principles and models. He operated with the simplistic "Sunburn" model of language learning: the student was exposed to foreign language patterns until he soaked them up (Lane, 1962). Typically, the materials utilized by Intensive Method programs and their New Key heirs—FSI, A-LM,* etc.—consist of dialogues which are to be "overlearned" through relentless repetition, pattern

---

*FSI refers to materials prepared by the Foreign Service Institute, Department of State; A-LM (*Audio-lingual Materials,* Harcourt, Brace, New York, 1961–65) is a series of materials destined for the high school level which follows FSI materials quite closely.

drills wherein structures are repeated and manipulated *ad nauseam,* and comprehension exercises in which lexical items and grammatical features presented in the dialogue and the pattern drills are recombined with a minimum of new lexical items. While materials prepared according to the "linguistic method" contain formal pronunciation drills—minimal pair oppositions and practice of phonemes in representative environments—pronunciation is acquired in shotgun fashion parallel with the memorization of the basic sentences of dialogues. In such sentences as *Je suis heureux de faire votre connaissance, Mademoiselle* [žœ swizoerœ dfervotrœkonesãs madmwazèl], it is difficult for the instructor to locate the exact source of the student difficulties since they may arise from faulty discrimination, improper differentiation, or simply short memory span; in sentences that may contain several points of phonologic interference, correction becomes sporadic and inconsistent.

The most serious shortcoming of these materials is that they constitute a closed system. The student learns a finite stock of basic sentences which he can parrot if the proper circumstances present themselves; at best the student can only be expected to vary by inserting lexical items in the slots of the pattern drills he has manipulated. Recent experiments in child-language acquisition suggest that human beings do not learn their first language by *mim-mem* (mimicry and memorization) but that they construct from their linguistic environment a model which can be projected beyond what has been heard in the past to form and recognize new combinations. Berko (1958), for instance, has shown that American preschool children and first graders can extend rules for noun plural formation to nonsense words with a high degree of accuracy; on the basis of *dog/dogs, cat/cats, horse/horses* they analogize *wug/wugs, fap/faps, gutch/gutches*. Similarly, on the basis of the productive *-er* verbs French children analogize *vous *disez* instead of *vous dites,* and on the basis of *ils boivent* construct *nous *boivons*. It is reasonable to posit that adult second language learning consists of more than the storing up of rehearsed utterances and involves the construction of a grammatical model on the basis of which utterances that have never been heard before can be "created". The construction of the model might be catalyzed by the artful presentation of material—for instance, contrastive pairs which point up generative processes—or, more simply, by the statement of *deductive* rules.

The New Key organization of subject matter and instruction follows literally the order of descriptive field work: first phonemic contrasts, then assimilation of forms through pattern drills, and last, translation exercises to learn syntactic features. Since the phonologic and morphophonemic structures of a language can be analyzed in terms of finite sets or lists readily discoverable by the analyst, New Key techniques lead to satisfactory assimilation and control at these two levels. Most pattern drills are of the substitution or correlation variety: the student is provided with a *basic sentence* and *cues* which are to be substituted in specified slots of the basic sentence. In correlation drills the substitution of an item in one slot is accompanied by an obligatory change in another. For example:

Substitution Drill

	Model	Student
Basic Sentence:	Necesitan más tiempo	Necesitan más tiempo
Cues:	Quieren	Quieren más tiempo
	Quiero	Quiero más tiempo
	Necesita	Necesita más tiempo

Correlation Drill

	Model	Student
Basic Sentence:	Necesita ud. el libro?	Necesita ud. el libro?
Cues:	uds.	Necesitan uds. el libro?
	nosotros	Necesitamos el libro?

In effect, this type of drill does not differ substantially from traditional conjugation and declension except that substitution and variation take place within complete utterances. Like traditional grammars, New Key materials present structure in exhaustive paradigms; such differences as occur are secondary in nature. For instance, compare the traditional and New Key presentation of a French present tense paradigm:

Traditional	*New Key*	
Je vais	Je vais à Paris	[véZ]
Tu vas	Tu vas à Paris	[vaZ]
Il (elle, on) va	Il (elle, on) va à Paris	[va]
Nous allons	Ils (elles) vont à Paris	[võT]
Vous allez	Vous allez à Paris	[aléZ]
Ils (elles) vont	Nous allons à Paris	[alõZ]

Admittedly, the New Key procedure reveals more accurately the structure of spoken French and is pedagogically more efficient, but a more radical and effective procedure would have been to present first only the forms in [v—], providing only the familiar second person and using *on* for first person plural; forms in [al—] would be drilled later. The ultimate objective of a foreign language course is to lead the student to generate all and only grammatically correct and stylistically congruent sentences in the foreign language. This ability presupposes previous assimilation of a finite set of grammatical patterns and a knowledge of the substitution possibilities within specific structural slots, but some provision must be made for the extension of patterns beyond the limits of drilled substitution possibilities. This suggests a very careful ordering of the subject matter to give priorities to patterns characterized by greatest generality—in French, verb forms manifesting the bare stem of one-stem verbs *(donne, donnes, donnent)* would obviously be presented before forms showing endings *(donnez, donnons)* and two-stem verbs *(finis/finissent; vend/vendent);* for the latter, priority would be given to [—*iss*—] verbs since these constitute a marginally productive class whereas the others make up a closed and residual list. Syntactic rules with high predictive potency, sometimes stated in semantic terms—despite the taboo that attaches to meaning among structural linguists—will have to be discovered and presented to the learner if, for instance in the teaching of English, he is to produce, say, *He tells me to do it* and *He asks me to do it*, but not **He says me to do it*.

Modification of the Teaching Context

New Key techniques and teaching materials, though unquestionably superior for audio-lingually oriented foreign language instruction than those following what we may term the Traditional Eclectic Method, because they do focus on the spoken language, rest on very shaky psycho-pedagogical grounds. Yet in the context of the Intensive Language Program, particularly as represented by the Army Language School and FSI, they were unquestionably extremely successful in producing, within a relatively short time, students highly proficient in the active use of a foreign language. Paradoxically, it was not primarily by the application of his specialized knowledge to the preparation of teaching materials and the elaboration of pedagogical techniques that the linguist devised effective programs of foreign language instruction. Rather, it was by the modification of the traditional teaching context. Since he viewed language as a complex aggregate of habits, he concluded that nothing short of relentless practice could lead to the internalization of these habits. Intensive Program courses, therefore, provided the student with constant practice and active participation through a massive number of contact hours, small classes, and readily available sources of authentic target language utterances, both live speakers and recorded materials. Typically, courses in the commonly taught languages (French, German, Italian, Spanish) at FSI provide for more than 450 hours of instruction in small groups of not more than six participants; the period of instruction for "exotic" languages is more than twice as long.

In Intensive Method programs contact was also intensified by the modification of the traditional foreign language teaching context: small classes, seldom containing more than ten students; variation in class size; specialization of teaching function, the linguist providing guidance and the native informant functioning as a drilling machine. In fact, in the Intensive Method the teacher disappeared from the classroom since neither the informant nor the supervising linguist possessed pedagogical experience or insight into the learning process. The Cornell University Division of Modern Languages program attempted the most notable modification of teaching context. The signal feature of the program was the variation of class size which accompanied specialization of teaching function: students met 2 hours weekly in large groups of about fifty for grammatical analysis conducted by a trained linguist generally of professorial rank; 3 hours weekly in a review "laboratory" section of twenty students where American graduate students, who had acquired insight into foreign language teaching by themselves having learned the target language, supervised the imitation of taped native models; and 3 hours weekly in a drill section of ten with a native speaker who presented new material, corrected pronunciation and directed drill and conversation.

When traditional foreign language teachers sought to apply the Intensive Program experience to high school and college foreign language instruction, they seized upon its tangible results: techniques, materials, and electromechanical devices, but failed to perceive that unless the use of new techniques and materials were accompanied by a reformulation of the teaching context and unless course objectives bore some realistic relation to the instructional time available, the New Key would fall flat.

Today the high school and college foreign language teacher is still forced into the straight-jacket of the elementary course. In fewer than 250 hours of contact, spread over a period of one to two years, he endeavors to introduce groups of twenty to thirty students to all the grammatical rules of the target language within a vocabulary of several thousand words so that those students who do not continue the study of the language—and these constitute the majority—will have at least a passing acquaintance with the subject matter. In order to complete the text by the end of the course, the teacher has no choice but to explicate grammar rules and to train students in the translation of target language texts into strained English. The happy few who do continue will be subjected to several levels of review grammar and reading courses, each of which will make attempts at exhaustive presentation, and remedial courses in pronunciation. Admittedly, it is utopian to hope that within the decade ahead, our administrators and our citizenry will become sufficiently enlightened to foreign language teaching needs to recognize that the easiest way to impart complete mastery of foreign languages is to institute the five to ten year sequences found almost universally in other Western countries. We must, therefore, improve foreign language teaching the hard way by increasing pedagogical efficiency. Clearly, pedagogical efficiency can neither be achieved by improved materials exclusively, nor by the installation of more complex electromechanical devices, but rather by the creation of a teaching context which will increase contact hours without substantially raising instructional costs.

The few adaptations of the Intensive Method within normal academic language courses have followed the model too literally and have failed to provide for a substantial increase of contact time. True, the teacher was converted into or replaced by a drilling machine—an imperfect one at that, since human beings can at best repeat rather than reduplicate utterances and they do lose patience occasionally, but the conventional administrative organization of foreign language instruction continued unchallenged: the subject matter was divided in terms of semesters—it should be noted, however, that at Cornell University language requirements were defined in terms of demonstrated proficiency rather than endurance —and classes were paced by rigorous course outlines which kept all students in lockstep and failed to provide for individual variations in linguistic aptitude, motivation, and background.

Recent and anticipated developments in electromechanical devices, the expansion of language laboratory installations, and the advent of the new field of programmed instruction make it imperative to experiment with more flexible administrative procedures and organizational frameworks. Patterns radically different from the present one-teacher one-class-room system are called for to permit instruction on a near-tutorial basis and to permit each student to progress at his own optimum pace.

Multiple-credit French

It has been suggested by A. Bruce Gaarder (1960) that the sole irreplaceable function of the foreign language teacher is elicitation of "graded, guided experiences in the natural use of the new tongue" and that all other tasks presently assumed by the teacher—initial presentation of material, explanation, drill, constant review, and testing—can be relegated to properly programmed electromechanical devices. Several research teams, notably those of F. Rand Morton at Lindenwood College, Missouri, and Stanley M. Sapon at the University of Rochester, N.Y., are developing completely self-instructional programs for audio-lingual foreign language skills and perfecting associated electronic equipment (see Hayes *et al.* for a report of these projects).

My own frustration in attempting to implement an uncompromising New Key program within existing administrative frameworks, first at the Pennsylvania State University and later at Indiana University, led me to design a program in elementary French which, while it falls short of realizing Morton's ideal, would provide the intensive contact essential to the acquisition of audio-lingual skills and permit progress at individual rates.

A research contract from the Language Development Section of the U.S. Office of Education enabled us to implement a suitable program and, for a period of three years starting in June 1961, to study the various factors and problems involved in fitting the program to the liberal arts curriculum and the foreign language instruction policies of a large university.

The experimental course, labeled Multiple Credit Intensive Audio-lingual Elementary French—hereafter referred to as MCEF—enables students to set their own rate of progress not only by providing them with a partially self-instructional recorded program and by freeing them from the conventional lockstep arrangement but particularly by permitting them to complete the course in any reasonable number of semesters and by awarding credit and grade on the basis of objectively determined terminal behavior in specific linguistic skills rather than on the basis of semesters successfully completed. MCEF is equivalent to the first three semesters of conventional introductory French courses, and participating students may receive a total of 15 semester hours of credit in from one to six or seven semesters. The only restriction is that, for simplicity of bookkeeping, credit is granted only at the end of a semester and in blocks of 5 semester hours. Grades range from A to C and students who fail to attain specified minimum scores in achievement examinations at the end of the semester or who fail to complete stipulated units of material receive an incomplete (I). Any of these students who fail to complete the course during the following semester receive a failing grade.

The course is now in its fourth year at Indiana University. On the basis of favorable initial results we are now trying it out at a small college—Culver-Stockton College, Canton, Mo.—and in a typical metropolitan high school—Patrick Henry High School, Minneapolis, Minnesota.

It was decided to test out the program on a sizeable group of average beginning French students rather than on a few specially selected subjects. Accordingly, each year a group of about sixty students, mostly freshmen, is selected at random from the group enrolling in the first semester French course, F101. Three sections containing the same number of students are chosen also at random from the fifteen conventional F101 sections and constitute the control group. The Carroll–Sapon prognostic test was administered to both experimental and control groups and fortunately, three times in succession, they proved to be comparable with regard to linguistic aptitude. At Culver-Stockton College and at Patrick Henry High School each control and experimental group contains from twenty to thirty students.

In a course designed for partial self-instruction and permitting maximum integration of the language laboratory with the classroom, how should the teaching team be constituted and what functions should the various members of the team assume?

The immediate utilitarian objectives of government-sponsored intensive courses and the reaction against the word-and-letter-oriented analytical bias of the grammar–translation method have led proponents of the New Key, and particularly its latter-day advocates, to interpret foreign language instruction purely in terms of the acquisition of verbal skills. But, as Mortimer Graves (Graves, 1951, p. 4) suggests, in the education of the man of the second half of the twentieth century, foreign language instruction has more transcending value:

> The educational purpose of studying this first foreign language is not primarily the mere acquisition of some useful control over it . . . but the extension of [the student's] language sophistication beyond the bounds of his own language and the mastery of techniques by which this kind of transfer can be made.

Formal point-by-point contrast between the structure and the cultural setting of the target and the native languages must find its place in foreign language instruction if the latter is to remain within the liberal arts and humanistic traditions. We decided, therefore, that MCEF should be a multifaceted scheme for foreign language instruction comprising at least three distinct components: (1) autotutorial acquisition of motor skills; (2) teacher-guided use of language in a simulated natural context; (3) linguistic and cultural contrastive analysis and general introduction to language as a social and formal phenomenon. This new interpretation of the foreign language teaching function necessitates numerous adaptive administrative changes as well as rigorous experimentation to determine, for instance, the optimum division of contact hours between the three components, optimum class size and physical facilities for each of the components, and the relative weight to be given to the skill and intellective aspects of foreign language instruction at various educational levels.

In the first run of MCEF, students enrolled for a minimum of ten 50-minute periods of instructional contact weekly; they were also encouraged to invest an additional five periods, on the grounds that a university student should devote at least 3 hours of class time and outside preparation for every hour of anticipated semester-hour of credit. Eight of the ten assigned periods were to be spent in autotutorial activities, one in two 25-minute Display Sessions (see below) attended by three students on the average, and one in lecture sections grouping all the members of an experimental class (thirty to sixty students).

Traditional introductory courses meet in groups of twenty students, five periods weekly, and two additional periods of language laboratory attendance are required.

Clearly, the differences in these two approaches to a basic foreign language course lie neither in intensity of actual instructor contact time nor in the relative competence of the instructional staff but in a redistribution of contact time and in a redefinition of instructor function.

Autotutorial Component

Students report in groups of thirty to a 35-position language laboratory equipped with dual-track machines and activated headsets and hooked up to a master console in two-way intercommunication. Tapes containing the recorded program are made available on a library system and students individually select any part of the program. At their language laboratory position, armed with a workbook, they listen to the program, vocalize as directed by the speakers on the tape, and receive immediate reinforcement in the form of echo or confirmation responses; they also automatically record their own responses which they could compare with the native model if they so desire.

Progress through an individual unit is paced by a series of self-tests. Depending on his score on each self-test, the student is either directed to proceed to the following section or shunted to an alternate review sequence. As soon as the student feels he has assimilated the material contained in a unit he is given a *Unit Test,* scored by his Display Session instructor; subsequently, the student has the opportunity to discuss his errors with the instructor who assigns specific review work when necessary. Autotutorial activities are monitored by specially trained laboratory assistants whose primary function is to note and evaluate students' accuracy of response to program directions, relative activity, and efficiency of work habits. They also attend to mechanical problems and record periodic random selections of student response.

Display Sessions

Primary instructor–student and student–student interaction takes place in small groups of two to five students, meeting for a total of 50 minutes weekly. Initially, students are assigned to Display Sessions on the basis of performance in a prognostic language aptitude battery (chiefly the Carroll–Sapon test) but there is occasional reshuffling to ensure homogeneity of student groupings. The Display Session, as the label suggests, gives the student an opportunity to use in near-natural and congruent context the linguistic structures assimilated in the autotutorial sessions. In the first run of MCEF, the students met in groups of three on the average twice weekly for 25-minute Display Sessions. As will appear below, other possibilities were subsequently tried.

Display Sessions are staffed by graduate teaching associates who, it is hoped, possess near-native fluency and accuracy but are not native speakers of French and who, optimally, have a knowledge of the structure of spoken French, particularly as it applies to the teaching of that language to American speakers. Display Session instructors are closely supervised and weekly staff meetings as well as visiting of classes by departmental supervisors provide some in-service training; the instructors also attend a 1-week orientation session prior to the start of each academic year. Display Session instructors have a slightly better control of spoken French, particularly at the pronunciation level, than instructors of the control (traditional) classes but their pedagogical training and insight—or lack of it—is quite comparable.

Lectures

Originally, the remaining period was devoted to formal discussion of linguistic structure, culture, and civilization in a lecture session attended by groups of thirty to sixty students. Although grammar and culture were presented inductively through dialogues, drills, and narrative material, it was believed, as was stated above, that the acquisition of objective attitudes toward language, training in the systematic observation of linguistic facts, and a formal introduction to French culture in the anthropological sense were legitimate by-products of a basic foreign language course. In retrospect, the Lecture Session represented a linguist's prejudiced effort to teach "about the language" rather than "the language" and constituted too slavish an adhesion to Intensive Method practices. Because of the self-pacing nature of the other components of the course, students soon showed a wide range of proficiency in knowledge of the structure of the language. It became difficult for the lecturer to maintain the interest of both extreme segments of the group. It was decided that all the factual knowledge presented during the lectures could be taught better through a self-instructional program using a programmed workbook as the principal presentation device, and that insights and attitudes could be imparted more effectively by the Display Session instructor. Consequently, in subsequent runs of the course the Lecture period was eliminated.

Materials

The successful use of the language laboratory as a teaching machine depends on the availability of materials suitable for self-instruction, that is, material programmed to some degree. No set of suitable programmed materials designed to teach spoken French was available when MCEF was instituted, and we were forced to devise our own. The program we first employed presented the fundamental phonological and grammatical features of spoken French, broken down into a graduated series of near-minimal steps and accompanied by congruent dialogue and narrative material; later units contained a program which trained students to spell on the basis of phonological and grammatical information and a series of reading selections which provided information on key aspects of French culture; the reading selections were accompanied by written exercises.

Essentially these materials followed the New Key closely and shared the latter's formal separation of components (dialogue, pronunciation drills, lexical manipulation drills, grammar drills, comprehension exercise, delay between audio presentation and representation in the conventional orthography) and its emphasis on *mim–mem* (mimicry and memorization).

In the Dialogue Exploitation Sequence, the students first listened to a short dialogue which contained instances of the grammar features to be drilled later in the Grammar Sequence. Next, the student was guided in the *reverse build-up* (Carroll, 1963) of the dialogue from syntactic partials. First, the English contextual equivalents were provided, but were then removed in the subsequent step.

When the students could provide English and then French equivalents immediately upon cue, they proceeded to manipulate the syntactic frames and the vocabulary items of the dialogue. The following *multiple substitution drill* (Valdman, 1960; Belasco, 1963) starts from the last sentence of the dialogue and alternately presents substitutions which are to be inserted in the Subject + Predicate + Adverbial Complement slots respectively.

Lexical Variation Drills

Multiple Substitution Drill 3

On est parti à minuit	We left at midnight
On est rentré . . .	We came back at midnight
. . . *tard*	We came back late
Ils ont téléphoné . . .	They telephoned late
. . . *avant-hier*	They telephoned the day before yesterday
On est parti . . .	We left the day before yesterday
. . . *à minuit*	We left at midnight

The final step in the Dialogue Exploitation Sequence consisted of a set of questions on the dialogue:

Questions on the Dialogue

	(Suggested answer)
Où est-ce qu'ils ont fait un tour?	Ils ont fait un tour à Saint-Germain
Est-ce qu'ils sont descendus dans une cave?	Oui, ils sont descendus dans une cave

Grammar was presented inductively in a three-step sequence: the student first performed *mim–mem* type Learning Drills, the grammatical feature, which he had learned, was then discussed in a *Grammar Statement* Section and, finally, his control of the feature was rendered automatic and tested by *Practice Drills* (Valdman, 1960). This procedure is illustrated below with the past indefinite *(passé composé)* verbs selecting *être* as auxiliary in Subject + Predicate + Adverbial Complement sentences:

Learning Drill 1

Il est parti ce matin	He left this morning
Il est rentré ...	He came back this morning
Il est mort ...	He died this morning
Il est né ...	He was born this morning
Il est venu ...	He came this morning
Il est sorti ...	He went out this morning
Il est retourné ...	He returned this morning
Il est parti ...	He left this morning

Learning Drill 2

Ils sont entrés par la fenêtre	They came in through the window
On est entré ...	We came in through the window
Elle est entrée ...	She came in through the window
Il est entré ...	He came in through the window
Elles sont entrées ...	They came in through the window
Ils sont entrés ...	They came in through the window

The grammar statement merely listed the verbs constituting the class and discussed the feature of agreement past participle–subject. The practice drills consisted primarily of correlation and transformation drills:

Practice Drill R—Correlation

Contrast *être/avoir*

(Confirmation)

Nous avons téléphoné
   ... sortis   Nous sommes sortis
   ... dansé   Nous avons dansé
   ... rentrés   Nous sommes rentrés

... partis	Nous sommes partis
... menti	Nous avons menti
... arrivés	Nous sommes arrivés
... travaillé	Nous avons travaillé

Practice Drill S—Correlation

Est-ce que vous êtes sorti à neuf heures?
... déjeuné ... ?
Est-ce que tu ... ?
... partis ... ?
Est-ce que nous ... ?
... atterri ... ?
Est-ce que vous ... ?
... arrive ... ?

Practice Drill U

Transformez au passé composé.
   Model: Elle ne descend pas
   Student: Elle n'est pas descendue
   Model: Elle n'est pas descendue

Il ne pleut pas	Il n'a pas plu
Il ne vend pas son chalet	Il n'a pas vendu son chalet
Elle ne va pas au chalet	Elle n'est pas allée au chalet
Il ne ment pas	Il n'a pas menti

While these materials proved compatible with partial self-instruction, their pedagogical efficiency left much to be desired, and they were revised for the second run of the course. The revised version departed from the New Key by a more thorough linguistic and pedagogical analysis of the structural elements presented: a distinction was made consistently between discrimination/comprehension and differentiation/production phases; the material was carefully graded and presented in minimal steps at all levels—phonology, spelling, grammar; structure was presented in terms of grammatical categories and generative processes rather than in terms of paradigms; for instance, the presentation of phonology was spread over thirty units, instead of eight, simultaneously with the introduction of vocabulary and grammar.

Productive grammatical features were introduced before residual ones (Valdman, 1963), and no effort was made to treat features, say, the negative transformation or the plural of nouns, in an exhaustive fashion or in complete paradigms upon first introduction.

Drill material was also made more natural and progressive: correlation and transformation drills were replaced by response drills which allowed the student to assimilate grammatical features by responding to a series of related questions posed by the voice on the tape and usually referring back to situations and using vocabulary presented in dialogues recently learned. Compare the following drills, also dealing with past verbal phrases constructed with *être* as auxiliary, with the sequence presented above (for the sake of brevity only the example for each set of eight items is given):

Step One

Answer the questions in the past tense.

    Model: Est-ce qu'il est parti ce matin?
    Student: Oui, il est parti ce matin.
    Conf.:   Oui, il est parti ce matin.

Step Two

Answer the questions in the past tense.

    Model: Il est allé au cinéma.
                  Et vous, est-ce que vous êtes allé au cinéma?
    Student: Oui, moi aussi, je suis allé au cinéma.
    Conf.:   Oui, moi aussi, je suis allé au cinéma.

The two previous sets of drills are *presentation sets* and were immediately followed by grammar rules and statements; thus the dichotomy—*min–men* learning drill and practice drill—was eliminated. The drill sets that followed the grammatical statement became progressively more difficult and reviewed previously drilled features.

Step Four

Answer in the negative.

Model:	Est-ce qu'ils sont arrivés?
Student:	Non, ils ne sont pas arrivés.
Conf.:	Non, ils ne sont pas arrivés.

Step Five

Answer the questions.

Model:	A quelle heure est-ce que vous êtes allés au bureau?
Student:	Nous sommes allés au bureau à deux heures.
Conf.:	Nous sommes allés au bureau à deux heures.

Step Seven

Model:	Ma soeur arrive ce soir. Et ta soeur?
Student:	Ma soeur est arrivée ce matin.
Conf.:	Ma soeur est arrivée ce matin.

Step Ten

Respond to the command.

Model:	Dites que vous êtes descendu au laboratoire.
Student:	Je suis descendu au laboratoire.
Conf.:	Je suis descendu au laboratoire.

The materials currently used with the third experimental group at Indiana University, as well as with the experimental groups at Culver-Stockton College and Patrick Henry High School, comprise a set of programmed units consisting of material presented in frames as well as drill sets: only features presented in the frames are formally programmed in chained sequences making use of standard prompting and vanishing techniques. The program is linear but students are shunted to preceding steps in the program if their response to criterion frames is not satisfactory with regard to specified features.

The New Key formal separation of components is totally eliminated: students are taught to discriminate and differentiate phonological features in meaningful utterances which also contain grammatical features and vocabulary items to be assimilated. The student is led to generalize from utterances he comprehends readily and produces fluently and accurately, and to spell their constituent elements by carefully ordered rules wherever possible. A few representative samples of the program are given below without comment; note that numbers refer to units and to frames within each unit; the portion of the frame appearing in italics is provided by the recorded program and is heard, not seen by the student. The word in the lefthand frame is the confirmation of the correct answer to the previous unit.

Sound Discrimination and Differentiation Sequence

	4.31 Is this a question? *Annick est la cousine de Jacques.*	Yes No
No	4.32 Which utterance is the French for "is"? [ey] [é]	First Second
Second	4.33 French [é] glides on. English [ey] is short and cut off.	True False
False	4.34 Which set of utterances is French? *say, day, jay* *c'est, dais, j'ai*	First Second

Second	4.35 The French vowel sound which appears in this set: *c'est, dais, j'ai* is represented by [é]. Circle [é].	[é]
[é]	4.36 Which French vowel sound appears in this set? *fait, c'est, mai*	(ü) [é]
[é]	4.37 Which French vowel sound appears in: *fut, su, lu*	[ ]

Pronunciation Practice Sequence

	13.282 The [p] of *père* is not followed by any:	
aspiration	13.283 Repeat *le père de Jacques* and write *le père*.	
le père	13.284 Answer aloud and write your answer. *Connais-tu son père?*	

Confirmation: *Oui, je connais son père.*

Oui, je connais son père.	13.285 Answer aloud and write out your answer. *Connais-tu le père de Jacques?*	

Confirmation: *Oui, je connais le père de Jacques.*

Oui, je connais le père de Jacques.	13.286 Answer aloud and write out your answer. *Veux-tu ton couteau?*	

Confirmation: *Oui, je veux mon couteau.*

Oui, je veux mon couteau.	13.287 Answer aloud and write out your answer. *Il passe le couteau à son père?*	

Confirmation: *Oui, il passe le couteau à son père.*

Oui, il passe
le couteau à
son père.

[ü]	4.43 Answer this question. Put one dash for each syllable in your answer. *Annick est la cousine de Jacques?*	

Confirmation: *Oui, Annick est la cousine de Jacques.*

— — — — — — — — —	4.44 Listen to this utterance as many times as you wish. Write the vowel sounds which appear in: *Suzy est la cousine de Jacques.*	[ ], [ ], [ ], [ ] [ ], [ ], [ ], [ ]

[ü], [i], [é], [a] [u], [i], [œ], [a]	4.45 Answer this question: *Suzy est la cousine de Jacques?*	

Confirmation: *Oui, Suzy est la cousine de Jacques.*

FOREIGN LANGUAGE LEARNING 99

Spelling Sequence

	5.53 Write the vowel sounds: *cousine*	[ ] [ ]
[u] [i]	5.54 The [z] sound between two vowel sounds is written *s*. Write *s*.	[u] [z] [i]
s	5.55 *Cousine.* The vowel sound *ou* is spelled *ou*. Copy the missing letters and repeat: *cousine*	c _ _ s i n e
c o u s i n e	5.56 Write the missing letters and repeat: *cousine*	c _ _ s _ n e
c o u s i n e	5.57 A [z] sound between two vowel sounds is written *s*.	True False
True	5.58 Write the missing letters and repeat: *cousine*	c _ _ _ _ n e
c o u s i n e	5.59 Write and repeat: *cousine*	_ _ _ _ _ _

c o u s i n e

Grammar Practice Sequence

	13.369 Answer aloud and write out your answer. *Vas-tu pêcher?*	
	Confirmation: *Oui, je vais pêcher.*	
Oui, je vais pêcher.	13.370 Answer aloud and write out your answer. *Veux-tu pêcher.*	
	Confirmation: *Oui, je veux pêcher.*	
Oui, je veux pêcher.	13.371 Answer aloud and write out your answer. *Veux-tu jouer au tennis.*	
	Confirmation: *Oui, je veux jouer au tennis.*	
Oui, je veux jouer au tennis.	13.372 Answer aloud and write out your answer. *Vas-tu jouer au tennis?*	
	Confirmation: *Oui, je vais jouer au tennis.*	
Oui, je vais jouer au tennis.	13.373 Give the French for "I want to play tennis."	
	Confirmation: *Je veux jouer au tennis.*	
Je veux jouer au tennis.	13.374 Give the French for "I am going to play tennis."	
	Confirmation: *Je vais jouer au tennis.*	
Je vais jouer au tennis.		

| | 13.389 Answer aloud and write out your answer.
Qui habite à Nice? (J) | |

Confirmation: *Jacques habite à Nice.*

| Jacques habite à Nice. | 13.390 Answer aloud and write out your answer.
Qui va habiter à Nice? (S) | |

Confirmation: *Suzy va habiter à Nice.*

| Suzy va habiter à Nice. | 13.391 Answer aloud and write out your answer.
Qui veux habiter à Nice? (J) | |

Confirmation: *Jacques veut habiter à Nice.*

| Paul veut habiter à Nice. | 13.392 Answer aloud and write out your answer.
Habites-tu à Nice? (Vichy) | |

Confirmation: *Non, j'habite à Vichy.*

Non, j'habite
à Vichy.

Evaluation

The preceding description of the design of the material developed and tested in MCEF reflects our opinion that the most important component of the course is individual autotutorial work in the language laboratory and that the success of the course is directly proportional to the degree of self-instruction that the materials make possible. It is important to note that in MCEF the student himself becomes the most important part of the teaching complex since he must assume the most demanding of the tasks previously performed by the native informant-linguist combination or the traditional teacher, namely, evaluating the accuracy of his oral responses. Partially self-instructional courses such as MCEF require the availability of audioactive equipment, but the student need not necessarily record his responses on a special student track, that is, the equipment need not be dual channel; any language laboratory where each student works individually from a tape played at his own position rather than from the master console, and where student microphone and earphone are electronically connected to provide for the audioactive feature, can function as a teaching machine.

The various alternative course designs which have proven effective, the very diverse nature of the administrative and pedagogical situations in which MCEF was attempted, and the relative simplicity and general availability of the electromechanical equipment it requires suggest that self-pacing foreign language courses can readily be introduced *today*. Breaking the lockstep feature and the administrative rigidity of current foreign language instruction does not require complex hardware or elaborate materials; rather, some clearer thinking is required about foreign language instructional objectives and a few concomitant administrative innovations: specifically, (1) on all levels of foreign language instruction we must concentrate on quality instead of quantity (Delattre, 1947); (2) "we must shift emphasis from *covering a relatively indefinite amount of language* within a definite amount of time to *assimilating a definite amount of language* within a relatively indefinite period of time" (Belasco *et al.*, 1963, p. 20); (3) we must define foreign language experience in terms of attested proficiency in specifically defined skills rather than in terms of years of study or semester credits earned.

The ultimate generalized adoption of MCEF or similar self-pacing foreign language courses depends on presenting convincing evidence that: (1) the normal student retention pattern is maintained; (2) it is compatible with higher-level courses; i.e., in addition to superior achievement in speaking and oral comprehension MCEF students must demonstrate reading, writing, and translation ability fairly comparable to that of students enrolled in corresponding traditional courses; (3) it can employ the type of personnel generally available at the university level (graduate teaching associates) and does not require any substantial staff increase.

It was feared that the novelty of the organizational structure of MCEF, compounded by its emphasis on audio-lingual skills, would offset the Hawthorne Effect and adversely affect student morale. Like most traditional language departments, the Indiana University Department of French and Italian stresses "reading" French texts of literary value as the primary pedagogical objective of the basic course sequence; audio-lingual proficiency is a secondary objective. The fate in second-year basic courses of a small pilot group initiated to the New Key in 1960–61 was a grim warning to students enrolled in MCEF that, in the short run at least, pronunciation accuracy and a high level of proficiency in spoken French did not pay off in terms of grades. We expected, therefore, a very high rate of attrition in the experimental sections. At Indiana University it has been established that 68 per cent of F101 (first semester) students re-enroll in F102 the following semester; retention rates beyond the first year have not been calculated. Experimental sections are demonstrating that, if anything, a self-pacing course can be expected to increase retention percentages. Higher retention rates on the part of MCEF students are no doubt due primarily to the fact that students who would fail the traditional courses are given grades of "Incomplete" and are allowed to catch up. The closer instructor-student relationship that characterizes MCEF may be another contributing factor.

How does the performance of MCEF students compare with that of students enrolled in traditional sections? It was established by the use of the Carroll–Sapon test as a pre-test measure that experimental and control groups were comparable with regard to language aptitude. Post-tests consisted of the MLA Foreign Language Proficiency Tests prepared by the Educational Testing Service, Princeton, N.J. The battery consists of four separate tests: Listening Comprehension, Reading Comprehension, Speaking, and Writing, and is given at two levels: the Lower Level Battery, aimed at two years of high school foreign language instruction or its equivalent, and the Higher Level Battery, aimed at four years of high school foreign language instruction or its equivalent. Although released for general use only in 1964 these tests are still biased toward traditional instruction and fail to measure skills that, in our opinion, determine audio-lingual proficiency. For instance, neither the Speaking nor the Listening Comprehension tests measure speed of response. The Listening Comprehension test uses written stimuli as the verification device, that is, students must demonstrate comprehension of auditory stimuli by selecting one of several written choices, and this is hardly valid for testing students who have had little contact with the written language. The Speaking tests overemphasize mimicry and oral response to pictorial stimuli and does not gauge oral response to complex auditory stimuli.

Beyond a doubt, however, the preliminary results indicate that properly programmed materials and students trained in self-evaluation can assume most of the foreign language teaching functions even in courses that stress audio-lingual skills.

Is the Teacher Necessary?

It has become a convention in discussions of self-instructional programs, on the one hand, to promise administrators reduced instructional costs, and on the other, to assuage teachers' fears of technological unemployment. MCEF was not designed to reduce instructional costs but merely to explore more rational uses of human teaching resources. Nevertheless, we are confident that not only will the course prove economically viable but it may even reduce teacher needs, since the use of a partially self-instructional set of materials reduces time devoted to class preparation and since staff economies may be achieved if a significant proportion of students can achieve required proficiencies in fewer than three semesters. But can most teachers presently staffing foreign language classes perform tasks that are beyond the capability of the machine (properly programmed, of course) and of the student?

It is generally assumed that a total control of the contrastive material of a language and fair imitation of secondary phonic features are acceptable minimum prerequisites for foreign language teaching at the elementary level, and that grammatical patterns and vocabulary can be acquired as one goes along. One year of experience with MCEF suggests, on the contrary, that the reverse priority of skills is required. Pronunciation inaccuracies on the part of Display Session instructors are undesirable not because the student who has intensive exposure to native models in the language laboratory risks being contaminated, but because the pronunciation deficiency slows up the instructor's rhythm of phonation. French conversation, being a private form of war, requires spontaneous and rapid-fire reactions among interlocutors, and, in this context, a 2-second silence can seem an eternity.

If the instructor is to involve the students in some sort of conversational activity and bring them to "behave" the language as they speak, he must produce sentences at a rapid rate that demands automaticity of generation. Unless the instructor has previously acquired the ability to generate grammatically correct and stylistically congruent sentences and only such sentences—and this represents a high level of achievement indeed—he will provide incorrect models for student analogies and teach "Frenglish", a language spoken in too many of our French classrooms, rather than elicit the genuine French taught by the autotutor.

In the elaboration of audio-lingual methods, we have come to remember belatedly that parroting basic sentences and performing mechanical pattern drill is not communication, i.e., the natural use of language in an authentic cultural context. Skillful elicitation of authentic conversation without straying from the confines of known patterns or succumbing to the temptation to explicate or drill is the mark of the experienced and gifted foreign language teacher and is precisely what the novice lacks. The most serious problem we have encountered in the elaboration of MCEF is that the best most of the foreign language teachers at our disposal could do was assume some of the functions that the programmed materials performed more satisfactorily: providing the native model, pronunciation and grammar drill, explication of structure, efficient testing. Lacking pedagogical training and proficiency in the target language, the teachers could not successfully lead the student to *use* the language in a near-natural context and stimulate him to *behave* the language. The minimum requirements that this ability seems to presuppose are a good though not necessarily native pronunciation, the ability to generate with automaticity grammatically correct and stylistically appropriate sentences in the target language, some insight into the learning process, a working knowledge of the structure of both the native and the target language, moderate wit and good humor, and the ability to interact and empathize with the students. Unless language teacher training and certification practices are revised so that foreign language teachers meeting these qualifications are made available in sufficient numbers at all levels, the machine will indeed take over, but the type of language instruction that will result will fall quite short of developing in our youth "a sense of values—personal, human, social—so that they may become discriminating, free individuals" (Mildenberger, 1962, p. 172).

References

BELASCO, SIMON (1963) Structural drill and the refinement principle, In F. W. Gravit and A. Valdman (eds.) *Structural Drill and the Language Laboratory*. A report of the third Indiana Language Laboratory Conference held at Indiana Univ., March 29–31, 1962. Publication No. 27 of the Indiana Univ. Research Center in Anthropology, Folklore, and Linguistics. (Published as Part III, **29**, No. 2, of *Int. J. Amer. Linguistics*, April 1963.)

BELASCO, SIMON, *et al.* (1963) The continuum: listening and speaking, In W. F. Bottiglia (ed.) *Current Issues in Language Teaching*. A report of the working committees of the 1963 Northeast Conference on the Teaching of Foreign Languages, Baltimore.

BERKO, JEAN (1958) The child's learning of English morphology, *Word*, **14**, 150–77.

BLOOMFIELD, LEONARD (1942) *Outline Guide for the Practical Study of Foreign Languages*, Linguistic Society of America, Baltimore.

CARROLL, JOHN B. (1963) A primer of programmed instruction in foreign language teaching, *Int. Rev. Applied Linguistics*, **1**, 115–41.

DELATTRE, PIERRE (1947) A technique of aural-oral approach: report on a University of Oklahoma experiment in teaching French, *French Review,* **20,** 238–50 and 311–24.

DESBERG, DAN, et al. (1961) *Foreign Service Institute Basic French,* U.S. Government Printing Office, Washington, D.C.

GAARDER, A. BRUCE (1960) Language laboratory techniques: the teacher and the language laboratory, In F. J. Oinas (ed.) *Language Teaching Today.* A report of the Language Laboratory Conference held at Indiana Univ., January 22–23, 1960. Publication No. 14 of the Indiana Univ. Research Center in Anthropology, Folklore, and Linguistics, October 1960. (Published as Part II, **26,** No. 4, of *Int. J. Amer. Linguistics,* October 1960.)

GRAVES, MORTIMER (1959) Languages in changing education, *Linguistic Reporter,* **1,** 3.

HALL, ROBERT A., Jr. (1950) *Leave Your Language Alone!* Linguistica, Ithaca. *Linguistics and Your Language* (1960) 2nd rev. ed., Doubleday Anchor Book A201, New York.

HAYES, ALFRED S., et al. (1963) *Language Laboratory Facilities,* U.S. Government Printing Office, Washington, D.C.

LANE, HARLAN (1962) Experimentation in the language classroom: guidelines and suggested procedures for the classroom teacher, *Language Learning,* **12,** 15–26.

MILDENBERGER, KENNETH W. Problems, perspectives, and projections, *Materials and Techniques for the Language Laboratory.* A report of the third Indiana Language Laboratory Conference held at Purdue Univ., March 23–25, 1961. Publication No. 18 of the Indiana Univ. Research Center in Anthropology, Folklore, and Linguistics. (Published as Part II, **28,** No. 1 of *Int. J. Amer. Linguistics,* January 1962.)

MOULTON, WILLIAM G. (1962) Linguistics and language teaching in the United States, 1940–1960, In C. Mohrmann, A. Sommerfelt, and J. Whatmough (eds.) *Trends in European and American Linguistics, 1930–1960, Spectrum,* Utrecht, Antwerp.

POLITZER, R. L. and STAUBACH, C. N. (1961) *Teaching Spanish: A Linguistic Orientation,* Ginn, Boston.

VALDMAN, ALBERT (1960) From structural analysis to pattern drill, *French Review,* **34,** 170–81.

VALDMAN, ALBERT (1963) Linguistic statement and language teaching. In H. G. Lunt (ed.) *Proceedings of the IX International Congress of Linguistics,* Mouton, The Hague, pp. 499–506.

CHAPTER V

*Programming Second Language Reading**

GEORGE A. C. SCHERER †

University of Colorado

THE rapidly growing enthusiasm for the audio-lingual approach to foreign language teaching, together with the dramatic expansion of language sequences in our schools, have made it imperative that the teaching of reading be subjected to very close scrutiny. Those of us who are convinced of the superiority of an audio-lingual beginning in foreign language teaching are not content simply to train illiterate polyglots. We must now exploit to the utmost the advantages of an audio-lingual beginning in the development of real reading ability as opposed to some sort of deciphering process. It is the purpose of this presentation to investigate some possibilities for building up a reading program in a systematic way, so that at the end of a four-year high school sequence the students will be prepared to read unabridged, unadapted, and unglossed modern literary works of moderate difficulty (Scherer *et al.*, 1963).

Prerequisites

The audio-lingual approach to second language teaching provides our students with two indispensable prerequisites for the development of real reading power. The first of these is the mastery of the

* Originally published in *Teacher's Notebook in Modern Foreign Languages*, Spring 1964, by School Department Research Division, Harcourt, Brace & World, 757 Third Ave., New York, N.Y. 10017. Copyright, 1964, by George A. C. Scherer. Reprinted by permission.

sound system. It is the contention here that real reading, whether silent or aloud, implies reading with the appropriate melody of the language—the proper tone, color, rhythm, music. We need only think of the reading of poetry in order to realize how important this is. A poem read with a distorted phonetic melody is no longer the author's creation. This is also true of superior prose. In fact, only in connection with the reading of scientific literature in the search for pure information could it perhaps be argued that the appropriate phonetic melody of the language is of little importance.

The assertion that the appropriate phonetic melody is important even in silent reading is supported by the theory of inner speech. Recent research has all but proven the validity of this theory, and it appears that it is quite safe now to assume its tenets. Everything, or almost everything, we read or think is verbalized innerly, in terms of what psychologists call silent or incipient speech. We can draw an analogy with the radio that is perfectly tuned but whose volume setting is so low that the message is inaudible. Inasmuch as the incipient articulatory movements for the actual speech sounds do, however, attend this silent speech, we can see how important it is to have full phonetic control of the language even for silent reading if complete appreciation of the author's style is our goal (Edfeldt, 1960; Sokolov, 1960).

The second indispensable prerequisite to the development of true reading power is the automatic and direct understanding of the structural patterns of the language from seeing their written representations. Again, the audio-lingual approach can provide the student with precisely this competence. After meaning is established, English is gradually banished from the student's mind by over-learning. Thus, when the reading of already overlearned audio-lingual material begins, the bond between the marks on paper (symbols) and the objects and concepts they represent (referents) is well established. The student then does not have to read indirectly, with mental translation into English, before the message has meaning. Direct association makes for faster reading because mental translation, even at so-called lightning speed, is a handicap. But even more important is the fact that full cultural meaning can never be achieved if the symbols from the first culture are used as the vehicles of meaning for the second, for the semantic range of the symbols of one language are never really equivalent to those of another. Our goal is to enable students to understand, to think, to speak, to read, and to write in each language without reference to the other (Lambert, 1961).

A Systematic Approach

Once we are satisfied that the student controls the total phonetic melody and a substantial number of the patterns of the second language, the problem of teaching reading is two-pronged: (1) The remainder of the basic patterns must be introduced and drilled to the point of automatic comprehension with direct association; and (2) the vocabulary must be expanded to include at least 5000 of the most frequent words in the language to be recognized for their meaning with direct association. Ideally, this is not too different from learning to read the native language, except that already acquired literacy in the mother tongue means that the early steps, such as learning to recognize the alphabet and a great variety of combinations of the individual letters, can be by-passed. At least this holds if we are dealing with a second language that employs the same alphabet as the first.

How, then, is this goal of reading with direct association to be achieved? It can be done by making use of one of the current psychological theories concerning the process of learning. "Programmed instruction" and "teaching machine" are terms with which teachers in every field are becoming familiar. Very often they imply the use of elaborate and expensive equipment. But programmed instruction need not depend upon machines; the principles of programmed instruction can readily be applied to the construction of language courses so that the book, in effect, becomes the "teaching machine".

The requirements of programmed instruction are simple and logical: (1) the desired "terminal behavior" must be clearly specified; (2) the material must be organized and presented so that progress is made by a sequence of small steps, each one made easier by the mastery of the last one; and (3) the student must have the opportunity to test himself at every step in the program.*

Terminal Behavior

Now let us see how these requirements for programmed instruction can be met in a foreign language reading program. The first one calls for a specification of the desired terminal behavior, that is, the skills, the knowledge, and the response tendencies that we wish to produce. Reading with direct association between word and concept, with eventual liberation from especially constructed and glossed material, is the terminal behavior which we wish to attain. This assumes the ability to recognize automatically at least 5000 words of high frequency and the ability to recognize automatically the basic grammatical structure of the language. If the student has *active* control of some or all of the vocabulary and grammar, so much the better.

Let us deal with the vocabulary problem first. The number of words needed is based on current experience with a team of textbook writers. It is now reasonably, though not yet absolutely, clear that about 5000 words will liberate the student. The choice of the words to be taught is not so clear. Ideally, it should be based on massive frequency counts of both the spoken and written language of the most modern times. (The reason for the emphasis on modern forms for our purposes will be discussed later.) Unfortunately, modern frequency lists of sufficient length—that is, covering 5000 or more words—are not yet available in most of the languages that concern us primarily, although some progress is being made here and there. In the meantime, we have no choice except to resort to the outdated and truncated older lists and to apply common sense in our selection of the valid terms and in the elimination of what has by now become uncommon. This is not an easy task because even the native speakers cannot be sure of the relative frequency of the words they use.

---

* The wording is approximately that of John B. Carroll, psychologist, Harvard University (Carroll, 1962).

In dealing with the issue of the lexical volume that should be known before liberated reading can take place, it would be helpful to have an unchallengeable definition of the concept "word". Although we cannot digress here to explore attempts to define it, perhaps we can at least suggest another approach which will suffice for a pedagogy of reading. For our purposes, it will help to focus on a definition of what a *new* word is: It is any lexical unit—that is, any word or expression—which is likely to cause the student to stop reading because adequate meaning is not immediately apparent. Of course, what is new and therefore a reading stoppage for one student may not be one for another, even though both have had exactly the same course of study. One student may readily grasp the meaning of a derived form while the other does not. For the first it is a known word; for the second it is an unknown word. The same thing applies to inferential possibilities: the first student may have trouble, while the second does not. In all of this, judgments as to what is likely to constitute a reading stoppage for the majority of students have to be exercised by the authors. Each such predicted stoppage must be counted as new and must, therefore, be glossed.

I have mentioned that at least an automatic passive control of all the grammatical elements is necessarily a part of the terminal behavior we wish to achieve, but that it is even better if some of the control is active as well. Since listening-speaking skill should be the fundamental axis of the entire language sequence, it seems efficient to separate the morphological and syntactical phenomena that are useful in everyday speech from those that are almost never employed by native speakers. Then each group of elements can be taught in a different way. The spoken patterns can be presented and drilled for active control, whereas those that are rarely heard except in formal lectures can be presented for automatic recognition only in reading and listening.

In specifying the terminal behavior required for liberated reading, I have tried to indicate that there are some difficulties, but I should also like to express the confidence that the main problems are being solved. Most of the problems still to be solved are in the area of the lexical inventory. The grammatical load is fairly obvious in terms both of its nature and its quantity. The native speakers can readily distinguish between the structures that are useful for speaking and those that need be taught passively only. It is fortunate, indeed, that the total number of structures is rather limited and therefore quite manageable. By comparison, the lexical inventory seems infinite.

Step-by-Step Organization

The second requirement for programmed instruction, namely, that the material must be organized and presented in a carefully designed progression of steps of appropriate size, can also be met in teaching second language reading. This is accomplished by introducing the new lexical and grammatical units at regular, evenly-spaced, and manageable intervals. The following five basic guidelines are suggested as a means of fulfilling this requirement as far as the vocabulary is concerned:

1. The density of new words should not exceed one new word in about every thirty-five running words or in every three or four lines of text in which everything else is known or too obvious to gloss. This careful spacing is essential if the habits of direct association which have been built up by the audio-lingual work are to be maintained. It is a formula which is based in part on the experiments of Michael West in the 1920's (West, 1926 and 1927). West, who was teaching English to Bengali students in India, discovered that one new word in every fifty running words was the most rapid introduction one could employ and still maintain the direct bond. But West was teaching English to speakers of a vastly different language. In the teaching of a second language more closely related to the first, the recognition problem is considerably simplified.

More recently the one-in-thirty-five formula was put to a test at the University of Colorado in a large-scale, highly controlled experiment comparing a traditional and an audio-lingual approach to the teaching of German (Scherer and Wertheimer, 1964). The formula of one new word in every thirty-five running words was applied in all of the readings for the audio-lingual classes. A variety of tests designed to assess the degree of direct association revealed that the experimental group had far better habits in this area than the matched control group. It is highly unlikely that this great difference was produced by the audio-lingual approach alone. In other words, if we had used unprogrammed reading material with the audio-lingual beginners we could have expected to destroy much of the direct association that had been built up by the time we taught them to read in the twelfth week of instruction.

2. The new words or expressions must be spaced as evenly as possible. If several new words must be introduced in a shorter space, there should be a compensating wider spread before another new item is introduced. A cluster of new words will tend to force the student to decode the entire passage into English equivalents—in other words, to translate.

3. The vocabulary must be as useful as possible. If the final goal of 5000 or more common words is to be achieved, the use of a word that has little chance of being repeated in other contexts is a luxury that cannot often be afforded. Synonyms are useful for glossing in the foreign language and they also offer stylistic advantages. However, they do not add to the story-telling power of the writer and should be used conservatively in the beginning when the writers need to add new concepts as rapidly as feasible.

4. Words that are obvious to the student need not be counted as new words, and will serve to bring the vocabulary forward more rapidly. For instance, true or reasonably true cognates and also loan words need not be regarded as new. However, they should be signaled by devices such as italics or asterisks as a part of the process of teaching the art of inference. Derived forms that are readily recognizable once the derivational system is known need not be counted against the formula. The presentation of derivational systems should begin as soon as there are enough examples to illustrate the patterns clearly. Names of places that are similar in the two languages and at the same time easily inferable from the context as being proper names can also be ignored in counting new words.

5. The language should be deliberately manipulated so as to set up as many inferential situations as possible. New words should be surrounded by contextual clues so that it is possible to infer the meaning. The student should be told not to refer to the glossary the moment a new word appears, but rather to try to infer its meaning. He should be told that clues to meaning may be found not only before but also after the new word. He should also be told to tolerate a certain amount of nebulousness and to let subsequent encounters with the new word bring it into sharper focus. At the same time the teacher must be patient and accept a certain amount of vagueness. Awareness of meaning will develop in this way more readily if English equivalents are not called for, since it is possible for a student to grasp approximate meaning without being able to give an exact and complete English equivalent.

As for the step-by-step procedure as far as the grammar is concerned, this is actually an inherent characteristic of any teaching approach that uses large quantities of new-type structure drills rather than chiefly composition exercises. The substitution, expansion, and transformation drills provided throughout a unit are designed to activate the several new grammatical patterns, one at a time. It can be argued, of course, that a dialogue or a series of basic sentences which may begin a new unit are the vehicles of far too much new material within relatively few lines to make them compatible with the principle of small steps that I have just outlined. This is certainly true if they are judged in isolation. But they cannot and must not be judged as entities. A dialogue at the beginning of a new unit is there partly to give the drills that follow some psychological ties with meaningful content. The dialogue is overlearned or even memorized—a feat with which youngsters have no real trouble—so that the drills that fix the new principles in new but related sentences can be mastered with comparative ease.

It is here, perhaps, that we find some of the most significant differences between audio-lingual and traditional approaches to language teaching. If the exercises in our traditional grammars had been more carefully designed—if they had had stronger content ties with meaningful discourse, if they had provided far more drill on each new principle, and if they had offered immediate reinforcement to accompany the exercises, that is, self-testing—the two approaches would not look so dissimilar today, except for the different emphasis on oral and aural work.

Self-testing

The third requirement of programmed instruction is that the student must be afforded the opportunity to test his mastery of each critical step as he proceeds. The most important area here is the lexical one. To the extent that it is feasible, each new word should be repeated two or three times as soon as possible after it is introduced. There are also other ways of achieving repetition. If a new word is glossed in the foreign language it can sometimes be repeated in the definition. Questions on the story can incorporate the new items. Other questions can be designed to elicit the new items, and if responses are provided, the desired practice with the new words will be assured. Words taught in basic sentences or dialogue preceding a reading selection should be repeated, of course, in the reading itself. In addition, new words should be repeated whenever possible in subsequent units.

There are some other ways in which self-testing and reinforcement take place. As a story unfolds, the reader is constantly indulging in a natural process of self-testing without any special aids. If the reading program is skillfully constructed, the reader will be successful in making direct associations, while at the same time reinforcing the previously learned material. Recombination readings—that is, readings in which only the familiar lexical and grammatical items are used to produce a new content—are particularly useful for the self-testing which leads to reinforcement.

The next type of self-testing and reinforcement is more artificial. It does not occur automatically, but it is stimulated by class procedures such as retelling the story or asking for answers to well-planned questions. Questions at the end of a story or chapter constitute a familiar method of testing responses. If suggested answers are also given, the student can check himself immediately, thus gaining the advantage of immediate reinforcement for a correct response. If his response is wrong, he can correct it immediately.

Another device is that of presenting questions in advance of the reading material. This prompts the reader on what to look for and tends to increase reading speed, especially if the question density is not too high. Care must be taken, however, that the students do not develop the habit of skimming to find only the answers to the questions.

The self-testing processes that have so far been mentioned are all directly linked only with the reading materials. There is an additional area of constant and effective self-testing and immediate reinforcement, namely, the pattern drills. Although they may, offhand, be thought of only in connection with oral–aural proficiency, their intimate relationship to reading proficiency can hardly be overestimated. This is especially true of the troublesome area of morphology. Pattern drills are the real key to bringing about automatic recognition of grammatical forms when the student turns to reading because every drill line is a test and every student response is followed by the correct answer. When presented on tape, these drills usually provide the student with the opportunity to repeat the correct answer after he hears the master voice. When used as a study device, the response to the drill line may be covered up, and as soon as the student has given his own response, either oral or written, he can immediately look at the correct response. Thus, whether correlated tapes are used, or whether some other use is made of pattern drills, they are perhaps the most effective answer to the third requirement of programming, that is, self-testing with immediate correction or reinforcement.

Construction Problems

We have seen that it is possible to construct a reading program that can meet all the basic requirements of "programmed instruction" as it is understood today. It now remains to see how such a reading program must be built up, first through the construction of reading materials which introduce vocabulary and grammar at a rate which the student can handle, and then through the selection, sequencing, and editing of suitable material from the literature of the language.

A few teachers still feel that all of the structures should be taught in the first two years because some students surrender the course after two years. A portion of these students will face such problems as entrance examinations for college and actual articulation with second-year college courses. This is all very true. But it is also an established fact by now that one cannot do justice to all the skills and all the grammar in the first two years. If by a block-and-tackle method all the grammar were pulled into a two-year sequence, the effect would be devastating as far as the building of the skills is concerned. There is a certain minimum of drill work needed to activate each grammatical point, and experience has clearly shown that at least three years are necessary to complete the work in high school. Two conditions would have to be met to make it possible to cover all of the grammar adequately in two years: (1) the language laboratory would have to be used as a library, that is, for some daily study outside of class hours; and (2) far more homework would have to be done than is now usually the case. Those teachers who can fulfil these two conditions may be able to cover one and one-half levels in each of the first two years. The others—the vast majority—ought to abandon the two-year strait-jacket and forget the notion that students have completed anything after only two years of study. They haven't.

In making the materials that bring the vocabulary and structures forward to the point where original literature can be used, the matter of choice is constantly haunting the writers. Two questions are ever present: (1) Which of the common words are the most useful and will permit the earliest transition to original selections? (2) Which of the structures are most important? The answers are best determined by first deciding on the earliest original selections to be used. By keeping a sharp eye on the lexical and grammatical features of these, the writers can steer a premeditated course into the first original selections.

Although some people object to adapting original works, it seems to be about the only way to build the bridge between contrived and liberated reading. Great care must be exercised, however, so as not to dilute content or to distort style to any disturbing degree. Collaboration between a cooperative professional writer and the textbook writers is one possible way of circumventing the practice of adapting. But there is little difference between compelling the professional writer to express his ideas in somewhat simplified language and having the textbook writer do it for him.

Experience has shown that it is quite feasible to make the transition to original texts with very little adapting and abridging somewhere near the 2000-word level and after about two-thirds of the structures have been taught. This point should come early in the third year of a four-year high school sequence. After the adapting of original works has begun in earnest, one of the most formidable tasks for the writers is that of building a substantial stockpile of selections that are closely compatible with all the requirements of the program. The writers become first of all talent scouts and secondly, adapters.

In adjusting the vocabulary of original selections, the programmer substitutes known words for uncommon unknown words and tries to maintain an even spacing of new words. Where such spacing is impossible without extensive alteration of the text, he devises other ways of handling them, such as incorporating them in the basic preparatory section. As the student is brought closer to the point of liberated reading, it is probably safe to relax the rules of programming gradually. Substitutions are made for surplus or unusual constructions, and troublesome phrases or clauses are dropped or simplified. The remainder of the unknowns may be presented in a preparatory section preceding the reading selection, along with the excess vocabulary.

The reason for such concern about the programming of vocabulary and morphology, while letting syntax come along in a more or less haphazard fashion, is based on scientific evidence that word order is much less of a problem to the reader than new words and inflections. This was proven long ago (Buswell, 1927) and confirmed more recently (Waterman, 1953) in studies of eye movements in foreign language reading. As long as the new lexical and morphological elements are learned systematically and directly, the reader's eyes move from left to right without any unusual regressions. The reading habits of direct readers are the same as those of native speakers.

While we think of pattern drills as devices designed chiefly to drill morphology, actually they provide an enormous amount of practice in syntactical manipulation. A pronoun substitution drill in Spanish, for example, that poses in succession the problem of making the verb agree with ten different subject pronouns in scrambled order, is at the same time drilling an identical syntax pattern ten times in succession. In addition, of course, much use is made of transformation drills, such as directed dialogue, and of expansion drills, such as adding adverbs to given sentences, all of which help to develop a strong sensitivity to contrastive patterns of word order. And since these drills are performed actively, it would indeed be amazing if word order should cause any difficulty in the passive activities of either reading or listening.

One of the serious problems the authors face is the proper sequencing of selections in accordance with lexical and structural difficulty. Long subordinate clauses in complex sentences are a strain on the memory span in foreign languages as well as in English. Therefore, the stylists who write simply, with many short independent clauses and coordinating conjunctions, should be introduced first. Judging this aspect of the material under consideration, as well as the matter of the density of new words, need not be entirely subjective. There are readability graphs that can be employed to measure structural and lexical difficulty. A very useful one, by Seth Spaulding, was first presented in 1951 to a meeting of the Central States Modern Language Teachers Association in Chicago (Spaulding, 1956).

The use of the graph is very simple: Count the new words of several 100-word passages in a potential selection and calculate the percentage of new words among the total running words. Next, count the number of independent clauses plus their dependents and calculate the average clause length. Then put a straightedge across the graph presented here and read the difficulty level on the middle scale. Of course, the graph will not reveal other aspects of difficulty, such as the level of abstraction or the degree of symbolism.

For this there is nothing that can replace the sound subjective judgment of the experienced teacher.

Readability Graph

Average Sentence Length*	Reading Difficulty		Vocabulary Density
4			
6			
8			
10			
12			0·00
14			0·01
16			0·01
18			0·02
20			0·03
22			0·04
24			
26	First	20	0·05
28	Primer	30	0·06
30	Level	40	0·07
32	Very	50	0·08
34	Easy	60	0·09
36	Easy	70	0·10
38	Fairly	80	0·11
40	Difficult	90	0·12
42		100	0·13
44	Difficult	110	0·14
46		120	0·15
48	Exceptionally	130	0·16

* Although Spaulding (1956) suggests the use of average *sentence* length, it is better for present purposes to use the average length of *independent clauses* (with their dependent elements). If this is done, however, the categories of readability, such as "easy", "difficult", etc., will automatically shrink somewhat, and "exceptionally difficult" will begin at a much lower numerical level on the center scale.

50	Difficult	140	0·17
52		150	0·18
54		160	0·19
56		170	0·20
58		180	0·21
60		190	0·22
62		200	0·23

Adapted from Seth Spaulding (1956).

The Reading Stages

It may be useful at this point to look at the problem of teaching reading in six successive stages from the very beginning to the point of complete liberation from an editor's help. For this purpose it is best to superimpose the stages of development upon a specific sequence in school. Let us, therefore, have a four-year sequence in high school, grades 9–12, serve as our frame of reference.

Reading stage I—the very first reading practice the student gets—follows a period of a number of weeks of audio-lingual, prereading instruction. The material read in Stage I is the same material the student has practiced, overlearned, or memorized before he had any printed material whatsoever in his hands. It may include not only the basic preparatory materials, such as dialogues or basic sentences, but also the drills that accompany these. It should include specific exercises designed to establish the sound–letter correspondences of the language. It goes without saying that during this stage some writing is also practiced, not only for its own sake, but for the sake of reinforcing reading skill as well. As new units are learned audio-lingually they can in turn be introduced for reading purposes, so that this first stage in reading can be practiced until the end of the first semester or even longer.

Reading stage II introduces the student to selections especially written for reading practice. However, at this stage the selections employ only the known lexical and grammatical items, which are recombined into fresh content. The amount of such recombination reading may vary from a few short selections to quite a number of pages. One of the natural limitations is that the constructors of the materials understandably find it rather difficult to recombine the severely limited unknowns into new material that is of sufficient interest to excite the student. This kind of reading, however, need not be dropped completely after the next stage begins. It can profitably be offered at various points in the program. As the lexical and grammatical inventories are augmented with future units, recombination readings in larger quantity and of better quality are easier to produce.

Reading stage III is the reading of contrived materials for the purpose of introducing new elements, especially new vocabulary, in accordance with the principles of programmed instruction previously outlined. It begins in the tenth grade and continues until the end of the year, perhaps even extending for a few weeks into the eleventh grade. Experience has shown that it is hardly possible to abandon this stage before the student controls a lexical inventory of 2000 or more words, and we also know that it requires at least all of Grades 9 and 10 to teach 2000 words. There seems to be only one alternative to teaching the first 2000 or so words through materials especially contrived by the textbook writers. This is to overadapt selections which happen to be fairly simple in their originally published form. However, such selections may not have much literary quality to begin with, and in drastic adaptation they will probably lose what little there was. A good textbook writer who is also a native speaker can usually do better on his own.

Reading stage IV is the stage during which adapted and/or abridged selections from the original published writings are employed. During this stage the vocabulary must be increased from about 2000 words to 5000 or more. The principles of programmed instruction should continue to be followed during this stage. Although many of the new words can be taught through word-building studies and the practice of analogizing these, the task is more difficult than it seems because of the semantic range of words. Whenever a word has two or more distinct categories of meaning, the effect is the same as the addition of new words over the 5000 needed. The student must be constantly encouraged to use his power of inference to determine the meanings of unknowns, and the teacher must in turn accept a tolerable degree of imprecision in this guesswork. Reading Stage IV will occupy us for most of the eleventh grade and all but the last few weeks of the twelfth.

Reading stage V is reached when abridged and adapted texts are no longer necessary to maintain the basic principles of programmed instruction. To be sure, an occasional violation of the rules may have to be committed if a policy of no abridgement and no adaptation is rigidly adhered to. In order to make this reading stage simulate liberated reading as closely as possible, the marginal glosses and the footnote helps ought to be omitted completely. This strategy also encourages guessing, which is needed as never before. Perhaps fifty or more pages of such reading ought to be included. Only two factors differentiate Stage V from the final stage, which is liberated reading. The first is the factor of selection. The editors will naturally be much more calculating in selecting the material for this exercise than the student would be if he were sent to the library to select an unglossed title that may appeal to him. The second factor is the presence in the book of an end-vocabulary for emergencies. There is a great difference between consulting an especially prepared end-vocabulary and consulting a dictionary based on whole libraries of material in many kinds of literature.

Reading Stage VI has arrived when the student can take an unadapted and unglossed book of moderate difficulty from the library shelf and read it for pleasure and profit and with direct association. He now has a large enough vocabulary to enable him to guess most of the unknowns. He has been liberated. For the rarer unknowns that will inevitably occur, and which he cannot possibly infer from the context, he will need a separate dictionary. At this point it should be possible for him to use a good monolingual dictionary instead of the usual bilingual type.

What I have just called Stage VI and treated as the final stage could be considered in terms of two separate steps. A block of readings, following the block for Stage V, could be included in the book for the twelfth grade without glossing the new words in the end-vocabulary. This final section of the text could be prefaced with a lesson on using the dictionary. A few of the new words from this nonglossed segment of the course, especially words whose meanings are hard to guess from their surrounding contexts, could become the words upon which the dictionary drills would focus. This would provide a realistic approach to the use of the dictionary in that the context, while not sufficient to make guessing possible, is still likely to be adequate to keep the student from selecting the wrong one of numerous dictionary meanings. The best definitions should, of course, be supplied in some way, so that the student is either corrected, if wrong, or reinforced, if right, without undue delay. If the drills are done in class, the teacher can supply the best choice in each case. At any rate, if the double step were initiated, Stage VI would differ from Stage V only in that the new words are omitted from the end-vocabulary. The factor of prejudiced selection by the editors would remain. Then, when the student selects his own unprepared title, he would actually be in what we might call *Reading Stage VII*. Even here, of course, he will not be making a completely free choice because the books in the school library will have been selected for their suitability for the age and ability level.

Quantity and Attributes

The number of pages of reading material required from the beginning of the adapting stage (Stage IV) until liberated reading is reached will certainly not be fewer than 450 or 500. We must not forget that if the formula of one new word in every thirty-five running words is maintained, only about seven to eight new words per page can be taught. Thus 400 pages would provide for about 3000 new words. But many of the words learned with only one meaning will appear again with an entirely different one. As previously mentioned, this increases the number of *meanings* to be taught substantially above 3000. However, the estimated 400 pages will probably still suffice for two reasons: (1) We have economized throughout by not using up any lines of text to teach the obvious cognates, loan words, and derived forms. (2) The basic introductory material for each unit introduces a good many of the new words in concentrated fashion. It is, therefore, quite conceivable that about

400 pages of reading material will achieve the desired goal. If we then add the two blocks of 40 to 50 pages each during the final steps before complete liberation from the editors, we are dealing with a corpus of half a thousand pages.

Now this may seem like an impossible amount of material for the student to read and, even more so, for the teacher to teach. But upon due reflection it should become clear that this is not at all the case. In the first place, the kind of reading advocated here comes very close to reading in the native language. Certainly no English teacher need hesitate to assign several times 500 pages in the eleventh and twelfth grades combined. One reason that the foreign-language teacher should not attempt *more* than 500 pages in the last two years is that considerable time during the entire third year, and perhaps during the fourth, must be devoted to the grammar that remains after the first two years. A second reason is that the skills of speaking, listening, and writing continue to consume their share of the available time. Still a third reason is that the new vocabulary, although strictly controlled, is far more dense for the student than in his readings in English.

The fear that so much material is too much to teach is also unfounded, for it does not have to be taught in the usual sense. If the books are carefully constructed, the actual reading can readily be assigned as homework and need not usurp any class time at all except for reading aloud to preserve the phonetic control which was developed long before. Much of the class time should, however, be given over to a treatment of the readings in foreign-language discussion. There can be no doubt that the students will be quite capable of engaging in this, and it is just as certain that the teacher is indispensable in this process. Stimulation toward active participation in the stream of speech requires leadership, and corrective work does too. The students will still be capable of error in pronunciation, in grammar, in choice of words, and in style.

So far I have said very little about the characteristics of the literary selections that should make up the large corpus of reading material needed from the beginning of adaptation early in Grade 11 to the end of Grade 12. It seems sensible first of all to concentrate on modern materials. If we can build a modern vocabulary of 5000 or more words, we will have given the boy or girl who surrenders his formal study of the language the best possible tool for further reading for pleasure or research. This also holds for modern structures. The student is most likely to want to deal with the present. If his research leads him into some older treatises he still has an effective tool.

On the other hand, the students who continue with the study of the language and embark upon a serious study of literature are also best served by a good control of the modern vocabulary and grammar. We can predict that all of these will do a considerable amount of reading in twentieth-century literature. I would even like to propose a drastic innovation in the junior survey course which most of these students will enter as freshmen in college. Instead of giving the course in the traditional fashion by beginning with the oldest masterpieces and thereby plunging the students into archaic vocabulary, grammar, and style, let us offer the course in reverse chronological order. This procedure would provide a kind of additional step in the overall programming process in that it would lead rather gradually into the vocabulary, idiomatic expressions, and styles of the past.

As for the nature of the modern readings that might be included in the program, there are several important considerations to be noted. The material must be of interest to secondary school students, but it dare not offend the Humane Society or the PTA. It seems safe to say that the most suitable material is that which is true to life, presents modern characters, offers a lot of action, and makes generous use of suspense. The level of abstraction must be kept relatively low, especially until we are well into the twelfth grade. Therefore, the greatest works of modern literature are not necessarily the best choices.

In any event, premature attempts to deal with the best of literature as an art form, rather than using good literature as practice material to improve reading skill, will not produce the kind of literary appreciation desired. There is no point in jeopardizing the student's progress toward the level of reading proficiency that will eventually make the serious study of literature as literature possible and fully enjoyable. In other words, it is suggested here that the high school sequence should concentrate on the indispensable prerequisite to the profitable study of literature, namely, control of the language.

The literary genres incorporated into the program should certainly be varied. The modern short story is an excellent category to begin with. Cultural essays and various types of journalistic prose are in order as soon as the vocabulary permits it. Manageable poetry should be included. And somewhere the program should offer a short play and a novella or a short novel. The important thing always is that every selection reflect the culture of the country concerned, not only in terms of authentic language, but also with respect to content.

Basic textbooks have often included readings in English on the culture of the country in question. This makes for a very convenient source of such material. However, there are some practical reasons for not doing this. In the first place every page devoted to English means one less page devoted to the foreign language; or every English page added means a higher price for the book. Secondly, class time devoted to the treatment of culture in English means less time for practice in the foreign language. Thirdly, there is a vast supply of cultural readings in English available. It would seem practical to purchase the material for the school library and use it as collateral readings. Written reports could be required or the material could be discussed in class in the foreign language, but it does not seem justifiable to take class time for English discussion of these. Much of this material is available in paperbacks and a rather sizable collection of different titles can be purchased for much less than the total of extra cost that English readings would add to every student copy of the basic text. Finally, programmed reading will, in a long sequence, lead to the point where cultural readings *in the foreign language* can readily be incorporated in the basic text.

Closing Statement

In conclusion, I must confess that some of what I have said is still theoretical and may not work out exactly as predicted when it comes to practical applications. However, I feel that we should have a theoretical system before progress in a practical system can be fully realized. Some reading materials fashioned according to the theoretical notions I have offered are already at the level of practical and functioning reality. We are in the middle of a language-teaching revolution. May it bring the results we all want!

References

BUSWELL, G. T. (1927) A laboratory study of the reading of modern foreign languages, In *Publications of the American and Canadian Committees on Modern Languages*, Vol. II, The Macmillan Co., New York.

CARROLL, JOHN B. (1962) What the FL teacher trainer or supervisor should know about programmed instruction in the foreign language field. Unpublished. Harvard Univ., Cambridge, Mass.

EDFELDT, AKE W. (1960) *Silent Speech and Silent Reading*, Chicago Univ. Press.

LAMBERT, WALLACE E. (Apr. 1961) Behavioral evidence for contrasting forms of bilingualism. Paper presented at the 12th Annual Round Table Meeting on Linguistics and Language Studies, Georgetown University, Washington, D.C.

SCHERER, GEORGE A. C., COVEY, DELVIN, ENTWISTLE, SHARON, HAYES, ALFRED S., LAMBERT, WALLACE E., OBRECHT, DEAN H. and ROBERTSON, BETTY (1963) Reading for meaning, In William B. Bottiglia (ed.) *Reports of the Working Committees, 1963 Northeast Conference on the Teaching of Foreign Languages*, pp. 22–60.

SCHERER, GEORGE A. C. and WERTHEIMER, MICHAEL (1964) *A Psycholinguistic Experiment in Foreign-language Teaching*, McGraw-Hill, New York.

SOKOLOV, ALEXANDER N. (1960) Silent speech in the study of foreign languages, *Voprosy Psichologii*, No. 5, 57–64.

SPAULDING, SETH (1956) A Spanish readability formula, *Modern Language J.*, **40**, 433–41.

WATERMAN, JOHN T. (1953) Reading patterns in German and English, *German Quarterly*, **26**, 225–7.

WEST, MICHAEL P. (1926) *Learning to Read a Foreign Language*, Longmans, London.

WEST, MICHAEL P. (1927) *The Construction of Reading Material for Teaching a Foreign Language*, Oxford Univ. Press, London.

CHAPTER VI

The Pauseless Tape in Programmed Pattern Drills

G. MATHIEU

California State College, Fullerton, California

WHENEVER a student practices with taped pattern drills, he should have a tape-recorder which allows him to lengthen the pauses by means of a pause lever operated by hand or, preferably, by foot (Mathieu, 1962). The pause lever provides for the implementation of the fourth principle of programmed learning, namely, that each student should have the opportunity to learn at his own rate. The speed with which learners of a foreign language are able to react verbally to spoken stimuli varies considerably and, indeed, changes during the learning period.

An experiment with native speakers of English demonstrated that even in the mother tongue the speed of response varied as much as 10 seconds. In an experimental drill, the subjects were requested to formulate a question according to a cue word from the sentence, "Paul gave Jane the book." After hearing the sentence, the subject was cued with "Paul", to which he was expected to reply, "Who gave Jane the book?" When cued with "Jane" or "book", he was to say "To whom did Paul give the book?" or "What did Paul give Jane?," respectively. After having practiced with three frames, the subjects' response time improved with subsequent frames, but still continued to vary from individual to individual according to factors which, I suspect, have their roots in hearing ability, fatigue, concentration, and just plain motivation and intelligence.

This experiment demonstrated that the response time for each individual varies and that it varies even within the same exercise. Most important, it became evident that the rate of variation is not caused exclusively by learning a new language because it occurs in the speaker's native language. But in learning a new language, the factors that determine response time are necessarily compounded.

Time as Cause for Nonperformance

According to the theory of programmed learning, the student must perform in order to learn. When the student is not given the opportunity to perform because of lack of time, as in the case of tapes in which the correct response is said by the tape before the student has had the time to begin or complete his response, we are violating the very principle of "performance at every step" upon which the entire theory of learning through practice is based. Inevitably the student will be frustrated. He has not been given a fair chance to do what he was asked to do, and this in turn will vitiate his opportunity to be "reinforced" and "rewarded" for correct performance. Moreover, when the new stimulus is heard immediately after the correct response, as in the case of three-cycle drills, the student's frustration is multiplied to the point where he is ready to give up completely and, if he can, kick the machine. In three-cycle drills, the student hardly has time to listen to and absorb the correct response before the new stimulus for the next frame is upon him. Consequently, the new stimulus falls on deaf ears, and as a result the student is unable to perform on the next frame. Small wonder that bedlam ensues with half-muttered and unfinished responses.

The *Teacher's Manual* for A-LM (1961) states that

> ... the silent space provided for the student to work in is just long enough for him to make the utterance required at the same pace as the model, and no longer. The purpose of the drills is not to give the student time to "figure it out" or even think briefly about what he is saying, but to develop correct speech habits—automatic, unthinking, correct response to a native speaker's stimulus—just like his English speech habits. It is only upon such a near-native set of habits that the higher near-native linguistic and literary skills can be built into the higher levels of the course.

While I agree with the principle of habit-forming exercises to attain "unthinking" performance in the automatic selection of sounds and structures (but not vocabulary), the blunt truth is that in practice it does not work. As pointed out above, even the native speaker does "figure out" whether to say "to whom did he give it" or "what did he give". And it is precisely in this area of selecting how to say what one has decided to say that variation appears in the time needed to make the decision. To be sure, the *A-LM Manual* suggests that "If the students hesitate or make many errors, the teacher stops the machine drill, gives the appropriate instruction and practice, and then returns to the machine drill. This procedure is kept up until a majority of students attain optimum performance."

I believe that there should be no dichotomy between practice for learning as provided by the teacher and by machine drill; I would therefore reverse the procedure and suggest that "the teacher stops the tape after each stimulus in order to give the student the time necessary to give the response, and releases the tape after the response has been given. He then rewinds to the beginning of the drill again and again until such time as the majority of students are able to perform in the pause provided." It is a self-evident truth that optimum performance can only be attained if the necessary time is provided to perform in the learning phase. Apparently, field experience with the three-cycle drills did not produce the desired results, because the tapes for *A-LM Level II* provide five-cycle drills in which the learner is given a pause for echoing the correct response, followed by the correct response again, after his own imitation. The "sandwich" system of enclosing the student's echo between two correct responses thus combines the advantages of the three- and four-cycle drills: the learner has the chance to imitate the correct response, to correct himself, and to be left with the acoustic impression of the model utterance, rather than his own, before proceeding to the next frame.

The following diagram illustrates the three types of drills and the spots at which the teacher or student should activate the pause lever. The example is a transformation drill, singular to plural, in a synthetic language.

Three-cycle Drill

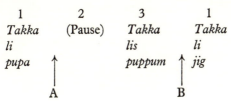

Four-cycle Drill

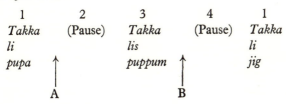

Five-cycle Drill

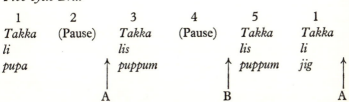

In all three drills (1) represents the stimulus said by the tape, (2) the recorded pause in which the student attempts to give the correct response, (3) the correct response said by the tape for correction or reinforcement, (4) the recorded pause for the student to echo the correct response he has just heard, and (5) the correct response again by the tape. In order to provide for the optimum learning situation, the teacher should activate the pause lever by hand or by foot at "A", after the stimulus, to *lengthen* the pause, and should hold it until the students have had the chance to say the response; at "B" the teacher should activate the pause lever to *insert* a pause in a Three-cycle Drill to provide time for the students to echo the correct response and, in a Five-cycle Drill, to *lengthen* the pause for the same purpose. A further refinement in the learning effectiveness consists in calling on an individual student for the creative phase after the initial stimulus (1) and on the group to echo the correct response after (3). Needless to say, the teacher will rewind the tape and repractice the drill immediately or on subsequent days until the students are able to perform in the allotted pause. But it is only the use of the pause lever in the learning phase that will eventually bring about the desired performance within the recorded pause.

One disadvantage still remains: the teacher-created pause at "A" or "B" will be followed by the prerecorded pause, causing considerable "dead air". This can be shortened by the teacher if, instead of holding the pause lever until the students have said the response, he merely holds it until they have *started* to say the response. The additional time will usually provide the right pause without too much "dead air". The student needs the time primarily at the onset of his response—he needs time to get started, but once launched, he may be able to carry through. This will, of course, depend upon the type of drill and whether the grammatical change the student is to make occurs in the beginning, middle, or end of the frame. In the choice between nonperformance due to lack of time and "dead air" due to a teacher-created pause, the latter would seem preferable in the total learning process. Nevertheless, for the ideal solution we must look to tapes without pauses.

Advantages of Pauseless Tapes

In a pauseless drill the stimulus and the response (Cycles 1 and 3) are recorded without any pause for either imitation or response but with just enough silent space—I call it a "hiatus"—for the teacher or the student to catch the end of the stimulus or correct response. Once a drill is recorded as a two-cycle exercise without pauses, it can be transformed into either a three- or a four-cycle drill by means of the pause lever.

Two-cycle Drill without Pauses

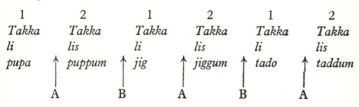

The teacher is now in full control: he can insert a pause at "A" to allow time for performance and he can insert a pause after "B" to allow time for echoing. If the students are performing accurately, he can omit the time for echoing at "B" and let the tape move on, or he can stop the tape only long enough to let the correct response "sink in" without echoing and then move on to the new stimulus. The same procedures are available to the student working alone in the "library" mode in the lab or at home with a tape-recorder. When listen-and-echo exercises, such as dialogues, are recorded without pauses, the same flexibility prevails. A dialogue can then be used either for listening practice during the initial presentation or in subsequent "warm-up" practice, or, by activating the pause lever, for imitation practice. A pauseless dialogue can also serve for dictation: the teacher can play the tape and stop it at intervals to allow for writing.

The chief objection to the pauseless tape might be that the student can no longer record his voice on the lower track for playback and self-evaluation. However, I would agree with Borglum (1959) that play-back by the beginning student is largely a waste of time unless it is done in a speech clinic situation with a teacher who diagnoses the errors of the individual and prescribes remedial exercises.

By Hand or by Foot?

For the most efficient and effective use of the pauseless tape, I favor the foot-activated pause lever. It has many advantages over the hand-activated one. The foot control leaves the teacher's hands free to conduct the class by hand signals for echoing or responding, for individual or choral performance. It also allows the tape to be locked at the spot where the teacher stops it: he can then leave the machine and walk to the student who needs special attention. Lastly, it appears that our reaction time in stopping the tape is quicker by foot than by hand, perhaps due to our training in driving automobiles.

The foot control is preferable for the student also. It leaves his hands free to write when working in the language lab with programmed materials that combine sound and sight (Mathieu, 1964). (See Fig. 10.) Moreover, by being compelled to listen attentively to the stimulus or correct response in order to stop the tape at the right moment, the student becomes engaged in a self-tutorial activity which challenges his continuous attention (Fig. 12). The same holds true for the teacher using the foot control when engaging in machine drill with his class: he, too, must listen closely, adapting the pace to the needs of the group (Fig. 11). And by being forced to listen to each stimulus and response, he undergoes a most intensive listening experience (instead of just a hearing experience) which should improve his own fluency. These, then, are some of the reasons for looking toward the day when all taped materials will be recorded without pauses. I am convinced that this will come about, if not for pedagogic reasons, then because the tapes will cost less than tapes with pauses!

References

BORGLUM, GEORGE (1959) Consign the mistake to oblivion, *Bay State Foreign Language Bulletin,* Vol. 4, No. 2, Dept. of Modern Languages, Univ. of Massachusetts, Amherst, Mass.

MATHIEU, G. (1962) The pause lever: key to self-pacing, *German Quarterly,* **35,** 318–21.

Fig. 10. An electrically activated foot control in the California State College at Fullerton Language Laboratory permits student to lengthen pauses to time required for echoing or responding.

Fig. 11. A student teacher practices machine drill with foot control in seminar on methodology at NDEA Institute at Northwestern University.

Fig. 12. Student engaged in homestudy with aid of foot control. After hearing taped stimulus, student stops tape, writes his response and says it. Then he releases tape to hear confirmatory response.

MATHIEU, G. (1964) Pause control: a device for self-pacing in the language lab, *Audiovisual Instruction,* June 1964. Every one of the thirty stations in the Language Laboratory at California State College at Fullerton is equipped with a foot control.

Teacher's Manual, A-LM, Level One (1961), Harcourt, Brace & World, New York, p. 32.

MATHIEU, G. (1965) The case for tapes without pauses, *Modern Language J.*, Vol. 49, No. 1, 40–43.

CHAPTER VII

Modern Greek Self-taught: First Step to a National Library

PAUL PIMSLEUR

The Ohio State University

IT IS the purpose of this paper to focus attention upon a national problem: *the urgent need for self-instructional materials in many of the world's languages.*

Trained Americans—diplomats, military personnel, economic advisers—must be sent to all quarters of the globe on affairs of government. In most cases, the jobs to which they are assigned can be better done by people who have achieved familiarity with the local languages, and in most cases the time available for training is very short.

The need for language training is equally imperative in the business world. Heightened competition for world markets has led the U.S. business community to establish numerous overseas bases of operations. The relations between American businessmen and their foreign counterparts, which touch at the core of economic power and are of a stable and continuing nature, exercise a potent influence in world affairs. The best antidote to an "ugly American" image in these relations is for the businessmen to acquire at least enough competence in the foreign language to meet the demands of courtesy.

Academia's need for rapid instruction in many languages is evident in its myriad scientific expeditions, international and area study programs, and individual research projects, as well as in connection with training for the Peace Corps and AID.

Is Adequate Language Instruction now Available?

It is not, as an examination of current facilities will show. College and university classes provide a means of study only for the common languages. To quote from a survey made by the Modern Language Association, "enrollments in 70 other languages (other than the big five), many of which are critically needed, such as Arabic, Chinese, Czech, Hindi, Swahili, and Tamil . . . accounted for 2·4 per cent of the total modern foreign language enrollment in 1961." The same source shows, for example, that only two universities taught Vietnamese; their combined enrollment was six students. Cambodian, spoken by three million people, was not taught at any university, nor was Somali, also spoken by three million people. It is clear that if an engineer, or an economist, or the wife of either, or a plain soldier or sailor, needed rapid training in Cambodian or Somali before going to his duty station there, he could not receive it at a college or university. Moreover, such courses as are offered are usually geared to the preparation of specialists over a two- or three-year period. What the student learns during the first few weeks or months will not help him very much to get along upon his arrival in the foreign country.

The Foreign Service Institute and the Army Language School—now the Defense Language Institute, East and West—offer excellent instruction of the intensive, live-with-it-all-day-for-six-months type. However, these schools serve only military and governmental personnel whose job directly requires fluency in the foreign language, and whose employer is willing to spare their services entirely for an extended period. These schools can offer no instruction to the business or academic communities, nor to the general public; they meet only a small fraction of the total language training requirement.

The problem is that of making excellent practical courses in many languages available to all Americans who need them, wherever they may reside. This can only be done by materials which are *self-instructional*. Therefore, some discussion is in order of the existing self-instructional materials.

The many language records now on the market—"Listen &

Learn", Cortina, Berlitz, Assimil, etc.—are not in the category of programmed instruction. That is, they make foreign language utterances *available* to the student, but do not *teach* them to him—the burden of learning the language rests with the student. Such materials achieve their objectives with the unusual individual who is so highly motivated and so highly skilled that he can teach the foreign language to himself.

"Speak and Read Modern Greek"

To meet the needs of adult learners about to go abroad, a project was undertaken to test the feasibility of a programmed solution to the national language-learning requirement. The result is a programmed course which is called *Speak and Read Modern Greek*.*

In April 1963, my wife and I went to Athens to spend our academic vacation pursuing a hunch. We wanted to investigate the possibilities of teaching the elementary stages of a foreign language entirely by tape recording. We determined to try it for Greek. If it worked for that language, we thought it would then probably be feasible to build gradually a national repository of programmed tapes, to make instruction in hundreds of languages available wherever needed.

We spent four months in Athens wrestling with the problem of programming modern Greek. Our aim was to teach American students to express their most immediate wants and needs upon arrival in Greece, and to enable them to read such signs, menus, and the like as are needed to "get around" in a foreign country. In daily consultation with native informants and experienced teachers of Greek to Americans, we established a priority list of essential vocabulary and structures. The problem was then to create a program which would give students the ability to use these words

* Twenty tape-recorded units plus Reading Booklet and instruction sheet, available from: American Institute for Research, 410 Amberson Ave., Pittsburgh, Pa. Similar courses in French and Spanish are available from Tapeway Inc., Box 3014, Columbus, Ohio.

and structures with easy automaticity; in short, to fuse the material into a series of challenging, interesting, and if possible even charming programs. They were designed to give the adult American student a maximum dose of useful Greek in return for every hour spent.

There was discouragement along the way. The seven units which had been written before we went to Greece had to be scrapped; the Greek they contained was correct, but socially inappropriate, because the informants hadn't been aware of what an *American* needs to know in Greece, as distinct from what every Greek knows. We had to go there to find this out for ourselves. Another source of discouragement was the seeming impossibility of teaching both vocabulary and structure in the brief half-hour we had allotted to each unit—until we found out that one could teach both, if (and only if) one organized the material so carefully that each piece of practice did double duty; the new vocabulary and the new structures had to reinforce each other, yet without violating the programmer's rule that each step (frame) be a minimal increment, within the student's grasp.

When we had about ten units ready, we set up a language laboratory and proceeded to try out the program with American students. While I continued to write further units, my wife spent 6 to 7 hours each day running subjects with the units we already had. All the students' responses were recorded and then tabulated. These data were used to find out what revisions were needed in the program. Twenty-five students, male and female, from 17 to 57 years of age, and of various levels of educational background were engaged in the project. We observed that the students seemed able to determine their own rate of progress without difficulty; the better ones rarely had to repeat a unit, the poorer ones did so two and sometimes three times, but apparently without embarrassment and certainly with final success, as their recordings showed. The students reported great satisfaction at being able to use what they had learned.

Evaluating this Greek experience, it seemed to us it had proved that self-instruction in a foreign language can be achieved. We felt especially encouraged by the faithfulness with which the students, whose attendance was, of course, entirely voluntary, kept coming back for more—even those who had to do each unit more than once. For future projects, we would recommend some increase in the length of the program. Also desirable would be the addition of a booklet containing essential information about the life of the country and what an American may expect to find there, particularly for countries where such information is hard to find in other sources.

The present twenty units of *Speak and Read Modern Greek* include a 200-word vocabulary of high utility and intensive drill in the use of basic structures, thus constituting an efficient introduction to the Greek language for pragmatic purposes, and providing a foundation for further study. The course teaches the student to generate correct and fluent utterances, sufficient to cope with pressing needs upon arrival in Greece—asking directions, ordering food, securing lodgings, calling a doctor, finding a restroom, making purchases, initiating social encounters, and recounting simple facts about himself and his family. Trained by the program to recombine elements he has learned, the student can produce a wide variety of utterances with a limited lexical stock. He can also read aloud any printed Greek word, and can recognize important street signs, store names, and danger signals. The course is designed to meet the needs of Americans about to visit Greece, who desire to acquire some knowledge of the Greek language in a brief period and by self-instructional means.

Features of the method

Granted the urgency of the need for foreign language programs, why is this particular method especially worthy of attention? What are its noteworthy features?

To begin, a word of caution. Claims regarding the efficacy of *any* teaching method must eventually face this crucial test: how good is the language proficiency of those who take it? A serious evaluation must correlate the answer to this question with the number of hours of study time needed to reach a given proficiency level and with the differing degrees of aptitude of the subjects. Steps have been taken to provide such an objective evaluation of the Greek program by allowing it to be tried out by the Foreign Service Institute, the Military Assistance Institute, the U.S. Office of Education, and the Defense Language Institute. This new evidence will supplement that acquired in Athens, where it was used by twenty-five American students during its construction period.

Yet, even before the results of the new tryouts are known, cogent practical advantages may be cited in favor of this programming method.

1. *The program has face validity.* That is, the teaching method resembles a well-organized language class. Consequently, teachers can accept and believe in it. As one expert put it, upon hearing the Greek program: "But I've seen this done in good language classes." The method puts a good language class, complete with a master teacher and two native informants, *into a box,* to make it available to everyone.

2. *The program teaches meaningful, useful utterances* from the first unit. The contents are selected to provide a maximum amount of usable language command for every half-hour the student devotes to it. This is in contrast with some other programs, which require him to spend many hours practicing so-called "building blocks" of language (isolated sound, meaningless syllables, low-frequency words) before he learns to say things he may actually need to say in the foreign country.

3. *The program develops generative power in the student.* It not only teaches him highly useful words, phrases, and structures, but also makes him proficient in *recombining* these to cope with new situations, thus getting the most mileage out of each item learned. The emphasis is not so much on getting the student to respond correctly in the learning situation, as on preparing him to respond automatically and flexibly to real-life situations. For example, when he is taught to say "excuse me" in Greek, he is soon expected to say it in response to a stimulus such as this: "Suppose you bumped into someone entering a store, what would you say?"

4. *The program prepares the student* to deal with the embarrassing situations he is sure to encounter in the foreign country, such as failure to understand and difficulty in producing a correct response. In this way, it minimizes the danger that embarrassment will keep him from meeting people.

5. *The sustained high motivation* produced by this programming method, as evidenced by the reaction of those who studied the Greek program, means that most students will derive more benefit because they will stick to it longer.

6. *The length of each unit,* just under a half-hour, is approximately that recommended by teaching specialists for a concentrated learning task. It is designed to fit on a 5-inch reel of tape or on one side of a long playing record, and requires no special "teaching machine" or other unusual equipment.

7. *Students trained by this method* can easily be phased into whatever other instruction may be available. By having them begin with this method, the short supply of competent teachers can be stretched and used to serve at more advanced levels.

Feasibility

(The Greek experience was meant as a test of feasibility—to encounter, under field conditions, the problems inherent in programming a language.) Is it possible for a trained programmer to prepare good materials for elementary instruction in a language with which he is not himself familiar? This is a necessary condition in any plan for programming a substantial number of languages within a reasonably short time.

Three kinds of competence are required to program a foreign language. One is that of the teacher-programmer, which includes the ability to organize and present material and sensitivity to the reaction of the learner—in short, applied educational psychology. The second competence is that of the applied linguist, who is able to absorb and, if need be, to produce grammatical (in the widest sense) analyses of the foreign language. The third is that of the native speaker, able to make correct and accent-free utterances in his language, and to supply information concerning their semantic and social implications. At least in theory the programmer need only possess the first of these requirements. In the present case, the programmer filled the first two requirements—applied educational psychologist and applied linguist. The third was provided by a number of native informants, some consulted for information about the language, some for their experience in teaching it to foreigners, some asked to lend their voices. This method was both workable and effective, and opens the way to programming other languages by similar collaboration.

Does the programming technique developed for the Greek language lend itself equally well to other languages? Greek was selected as a demonstration language largely because its vocabulary is almost entirely strange to American ears; the number of cognates and loan-words is small among the initial, high-frequency vocabulary items. Moreover, the Greek verb system is quite different from the English and constitutes a challenge to teacher and student. On the other hand, the phonology of modern Greek is not particularly difficult for Americans. Nor does Greek syntax appear to pose grave problems, at least at the elementary level to which the present program is restricted. Certainly there are many languages whose phonology and syntax are far more difficult.

Some additional evidence of the effectiveness of programmed instruction in the face of pronunciation problems is provided by the author's recent project to program French in a similar manner. French phonology, reputed for its difficulty, turned out to be quite amenable to the programmed approach—provided the goal is that students shall learn to observe all the phonemic distinctions of French, so as to be easily comprehensible and non-ridiculous, but shall not be expected to sound like native Frenchmen.

Perhaps the most challenging problems will arise in the area of semantics, as it becomes necessary, for some languages, to train American students to adopt the profoundly different world-view reflected in the new vocabulary they are learning. In all events, the best evidence so far obtained indicates the Greek programming method can be applied to a great many languages with good expectation of success. No language seems, *a priori*, entirely unamenable to this self-instructional approach.

Conclusion

To return to the original proposition: there exists an urgent national need for self-instructional materials in many of the world's languages. To answer this need, a national library or repository of such materials must be established. The initial project described here, which used modern Greek as a demonstration language, fulfilled several of the necessary conditions to the establishment of such a library.

(1) It has demonstrated that effective elementary teaching materials in foreign languages can be prepared by a trained programmer working with native informants. (2) It has devised a programming technique bearing resemblance to well-conducted intensive language classes; the high motivational value of this method has been demonstrated; its efficacy with students of different degrees of ability is presently under expert examination. (3) The method appears applicable, *mutatis mutandis*, to a large number and variety of languages.

A very large number of languages are described as "critical" by various authorities: the Voegelin (Indiana University) list shows 134 languages spoken by one million people or more; the Frith (FSI) list shows 154 languages presently considered most important to teach to government personnel; the Ferguson (CAL) list contains 275 languages selected by the Center "for their socio-political importance from an American point of view". These figures must be doubled if one wishes to consider teaching English to speakers of each foreign language.

It is concluded from these considerations, that a project must be brought into existence which will devote itself, with all due speed, to producing a library of self-instructional programs in many of the world's languages. The magnitude of the task urges that it begin without delay.

CHAPTER VIII

Closing the Circle: Training the Teachers' Teachers

JACK M. STEIN
Harvard University

THE training of foreign language teachers encompasses—or *should* encompass—a broad span, extending from foreign languages in the elementary school (FLES) to Ph.D. Great strides have been made in recent years, thanks to the Foreign Language Program (FLP) of the Modern Language Association (MLA) and the National Defense Education Act (NDEA), in New Key training or retraining of precollege teachers. Most of this has been done in NDEA remedial summer institutes whose staffs consist primarily of college language teachers, so that the institutes have had some impact on regular college programs as well. Up to the present, the only segment which has remained largely unaffected by the new movement in language teaching are graduate programs leading to the Ph.D.

The movement is strongest in secondary schools, and for good reasons. This is the area on which the NDEA and the U.S. Office of Education, with strong assistance from the FLP, have focused their attention, and a continuing retraining program of massive proportions, now in its eighth year, has had excellent results. Perhaps the most indubitable proof of this is the recent appearance of excellent text materials for secondary schools, commercially and competitively produced. Private publishers would not invest large sums of money in such materials (comprising texts, tapes, records, teachers' manuals, special tests, flash cards, etc.) if there were not sufficient demand to make them profitable, and the existence and widespread adoption of these materials has already provided a firm basis for a sturdy growth of the new techniques in secondary schools.

In the retraining of secondary school teachers, therefore, we have made a good start and a wise one. This was the ideal place to begin. For the retraining of the secondary school teacher is the most concrete, most concentrated, and least complex of the many problems which face us. On that level, the problem of teaching foreign languages is not complicated, as it is in college, by the strong literary or pre-professional student interests. All concerned can joyfully concentrate on language teaching procedures alone. But up to now the major emphasis has been on an emergency situation—the *re*training of teachers. Until the central thrust is toward *training,* the situation must still be looked on as remedial. Training teachers "wrong" (to over-simplify for a moment) in the first place, and then retraining them after they are in service is obviously an inefficient procedure.

In all other areas, we are farther from success. Foreign languages in the elementary school (FLES) are still in their infancy, if I may be pardoned the play on words. Techniques here are more controversial, and the numbers involved are still too small to encourage commercial publishers to produce FLES texts for the open market. Thus, neither techniques nor materials are as firmly established as on the secondary school level. At the other end of the spectrum, graduate programs, attention is only beginning to focus on problems of teacher training. Good reasons exist for this delay, and we will have more to say on this later. But whatever the reasons, the new movement has now reached the point where it must make its influence felt in graduate school programs.

On first thought, pedagogy, methods, materials, etc., might seem less crucial on the Ph.D. level. But a little reflection will show that in the long run the Ph.D. program lies, not on the periphery of the teacher training problem, but at its very source. For the FLES and secondary school teachers get their training as college undergraduates, and college teachers (the future precollege teachers' teachers) are trained (or not trained) exclusively in graduate schools. Therefore, as long as the graduate programs continue to produce teachers who have little or no understanding of recent philosophies and techniques of foreign language teaching, these teachers will be incapable of transmitting them to a younger generation, who then must be *re*trained at a later date if they are to be acquainted with modern procedures. (This is exactly what the institutes have been doing.) Thus the whole cycle *begins* in the graduate school. Modern techniques can hope to have a really firm footing in the foreign language profession only when Ph.D.s with a clear understanding of and commitment to them are produced. This cannot occur if their graduate program, by implication, omission, or downright last-ditch opposition, has failed to prepare them properly, or worse, prejudiced them against it. And at the moment this is the *status quo*.

It would be very fine if there were an easy solution and the task was simply to publicize and implement it. But the graduate school problem is the most complex of all; or rather, it becomes complex as soon as the element of training to teach foreign languages is injected. There is little disagreement in the profession that the college teacher, whether he teaches elementary or advanced courses, must be a scholar-teacher, and to this end, he must undergo intensive and rigorous scholarly training during his graduate years. And intensive scholarly training is what he does get—though there is reason to question whether our present practices are efficient even in this regard. Recent reports from various qualified agencies, the Association of Graduate Schools among them,[1] have expressed concern. Nonetheless, a problem of greater urgency is the fact that most of our present graduate programs for scholar-teachers ignore the problems of teaching.

There is some real opposition to doing anything about this. One still hears all too often the opinion that teachers are born, not made; that training teachers is useless, for the good ones don't need it, and it won't do the poor ones any good anyway. Such an argument is a plea for amateurism. No one who thinks professionally about our responsibilities could use it. Fortunately for the health of the nation, the medical profession does not feel this way about doctors. Nor would civil chaos be long in coming if the legal profession thought lawyers were born, not made. That this is said in the teaching profession is, I think, an indication of how far we are from a sense of professionalism comparable to that of physicians and lawyers. And I believe it reflects a desire, a subconscious desire at least, to avoid this very serious responsibility.

Moves have been made in recent years at one or the other university to act on this need, but in most graduate departments scholarly hegemony has such hoary prestige that recent gestures made toward preparation for college teaching can be considered no more than first steps, and timid ones at that. Behind the reluctance of graduate departments to move into this area is a largely unexamined feeling that too much attention to pedagogical and practical teaching matters is beneath the dignity of graduate professors and students alike. There are indeed many scholars whose interests and abilities lie far from the area of teacher preparation, but this is surely no justification for denying the student the professional training he sorely needs. Those who feel it to be outside their sphere of interest and competence should properly stay clear of it themselves, but they have the solemn obligation to see that such training is provided by someone who is willing and able to do so.

A better reason for hesitation is the concern that any increase in attention to matters of teaching would have to be made at the expense of the already hard-pressed scholarly training, which, it is argued, has been condensed to its irreducible minimum. True, a graduate program so transformed that it became principally a teacher-training program would not deserve the privilege of bestowing doctoral degrees. But there are few, if any, in the profession who would welcome this, and there is surely little danger that such an imbalance would soon replace the heavy imbalance to the opposite extreme which exists today.

We can train the scholar well in three or four years, given a carefully planned and thoughtfully integrated program. In the same amount of time or less we could thoroughly train a teacher. To attempt to do both simultaneously—and to produce the scholar-teacher worthy of both parts of the name we *must* do both—we are faced with the necessity of compromise. The training of the scholar, being a more rigorous and complex process, should clearly command most of the department's and the students' energies. Though the training of the teacher must not be neglected, as it is now, it must not encroach too seriously on the scholarly activities of either the graduate student or his professors.

In the long run, much could be gained by a searching revision of the entire Ph.D. program in foreign languages to adapt it to present needs. Until the profession is ready to undertake the kind of revision suggested in the MacAllister report,[2] strategy as well as common sense dictate that we begin more modestly. We must first develop a teacher-preparation program reduced to essentials, a program which can be of maximum benefit to the student in a minimum amount of time. This is a major task, and the remainder of the present article will be addressed to concrete proposals. Interspersed where appropriate will be descriptions of what is being done currently in the German Department at Harvard, which, for the past eight years, has been attempting to develop just such a minimum program of maximum benefit.

First I would urge that no student in his first year of graduate work be put in charge of a group of undergraduates studying elementary or intermediate foreign languages. That untrained beginners at the very outset of their graduate study are used as teachers of college freshman classes in most universities has been called a national scandal by a responsible member of our profession. The disparity between what could be considered even minimum standards of acceptability and what is actually practiced in this matter is so wide that only our familiarity with it prevents us from being profoundly shocked. I recognize that to abandon this practice would create financial problems, but it is surely not the function of the foreign language departments to engage in marginal educational practices in order to save the university money, and I shall mention later possible means of overcoming the financial difficulty.

If the graduate student were freed from teaching during his first year, he could instead pursue a full year's training course without taking additional time away from his scholarly studies. Such a course could include an introduction to descriptive linguistics, with emphasis on its relevance to second-language learning;

methods of teaching at all undergraduate levels; planned observation of model classes by the students; training in laboratory techniques; detailed examination of materials, including textbooks, workbooks, laboratory exercises, visual aids, and the like; and—another important ingredient overlooked in present graduate programs—lectures and discussions on the present state and development of the foreign language teaching profession.

First-year graduate students in German at Harvard must take a full graduate program and are not allowed to become teaching fellows. This is a strong feature of our program, for it permits the student to get a concentrated start on his regular graduate work and at the same time makes it possible for us to require a course in teaching during his first year. The MacAllister report recommends that the "methods" course be given concurrently with the beginning of teaching.[2] Though we can see some gain in this, we can see more loss, at least in the context of graduate programs as they now exist. In the first place, a first-year student who must take a graduate course in teaching and in addition teach a section (often more than one) of elementary German has too little time for his other graduate responsibilities. Furthermore, though he gets his training concurrently, he starts his teaching as an utter neophyte, with no real sense of the principles and techniques involved, and this is far from ideal.

At Harvard, Germanic Philology 280, "The German Language and the Teaching of German", is offered each fall semester, and required of every graduate student who expects later to become a teaching fellow in our department. It is the keystone of our training program and is designed to acquaint the student with the theory and the specific practice of our own language courses, in preparation for his function as a teaching fellow, and, on a broader scale, to introduce him to the profession which he is preparing to enter. The subject matter of the course falls into three unequal subdivisions. Part One, taking approximately a third of the total time, introduces the student to the linguistic scientist's view of language. An important aim is to counteract the traditional notions on language acquired by most of the students in their high school and college English (and, alas, also in their foreign language) classes. For this purpose,

CLOSING THE CIRCLE

we begin with Robert Hall's provocative *Linguistics and Your Language*.[3] The whole book is read. Numerous assertions in it are debated hotly, often attacked vehemently by the students, and defended by the teacher, who relates them to the broad principles of the linguist's view of language. Gleason,[4] and Hockett,[5] as well as Sapir's *Language*,[6] are used as supplementary reading to add detail in certain instances, but they are subordinated to Hall as the main text, since the course is not, and does not intend to be, an introduction to linguistics. It deals only with what is deemed necessary for an American teacher of German to know about the new theory of language in order to teach a good elementary or intermediate class according to effective modern teaching procedures. Only the very basic linguistic terminology is used. Phonetic symbols are discussed and practiced, and phonemes, intonation patterns, and morphemes are explained, but in a manner far more summary, condensed and elementary than would be proper in a linguistics course. In every aspect, inclusion or exclusion of material is determined by whether the information is useful for the teacher of elementary and intermediate German. The recent Moulton[7] and Kufner[8] contrastive studies, two volumes produced solely with this in mind, are also required texts. The five films on language produced by the MLA's Center for Applied Linguistics[9] are shown and discussed during the semester.

Part Two of the course occupies about half the total time of the semester. Here the varieties of methods of elementary foreign language instruction, i.e. grammar-translation, direct, natural, reading, etc., are first listed and defined, and it is demonstrated how the implementation of the view of language we have just finished examining results in the audio-lingual method *and no other*. We then proceed with a detailed examination of grammars. This is the most critical phase of the entire course, for an ability to judge a grammar text professionally is a critical skill. Five or six grammars are examined. The students are required to evaluate in detail all the front matter and Lessons One through Three plus one or two selected lessons from later in the book. The discussion in class during the weeks this is being done is always potent and confronts basic principles in their practical application, which are often more accessible and meaningful to the students than the theory alone. In the introductory presentation of the various alternative methods, their strengths and also their venerability are pointed out, and the fact that historically most foreign language learning has been done in one of these ways is stressed. Examination of current grammars shows, however, that for practical purposes, the teacher does not have a choice among these various methods; available materials (among American texts, at least) cluster around either the audio-lingual or the "traditional" eclectic approach. With this juxtaposition, it is easy to establish the superiority of the audio-lingual texts.

After examination and discussion of the grammars, arrangements are made for each student to make one or more visits to a section of an undergraduate elementary audio-lingual course taught by an experienced teacher. The latter is informed of exactly when his visitors are coming, so that, without departing from his usual procedures, he can show them as wide a variety of techniques as is feasible. Although time for subsequent discussion of these visiting experiences is provided, usually not much is said. The students have seen the audio-lingual approach in action, it fits together with the contents of the course they are taking, and they are satisfied. The kind of subtleties which could be brought up by experienced teachers are still, for the most part, beyond their perception at this early stage. A similar procedure, including close examination of texts and subsequent visits to classes, then follows for intermediate German.

After this comes relatively brief (all too brief) attention to the language laboratory, including demonstration and discussion of sample tapes. There is little or no discussion of more advanced language and literature courses. Not only lack of time accounts for this omission, however. We believe that this teachers' course, to be successful, must convey a sense of immediacy and practicality, and the burning issue for these first-year graduate students is preparation for the teaching which will be expected of them the following year (and for how many years after that?). Advanced language and literature courses lie for them in the distant future.

The remainder of the semester is devoted to more general professional matters. A year's run of each of the leading pedagogical journals (including *PMLA*) is examined, reported on, and discussed. In the final week, *The National Interest and Foreign Languages*[10] is read, and details regarding NDEA, FLP, AATG (American Association of Teachers of German), etc., are supplied. The final words are directed to the college German teacher as a split personality, that is, a Germanist with a research specialty in the field of literature or philology, who must also command the techniques of successful elementary and intermediate language instruction. The absence from the course of a history of foreign language instruction (except for what is in *The National Interest and Foreign Languages*[10]) as well as such topics as the psychology of learning (in the abstract) and other staples of education courses is deliberate. Our graduate students, for the most part, are more excited about their regular Ph.D. courses and subject matter than they are about teaching matters. This predilection is understandable, is real, and must be taken into consideration in our planning. Furthermore, our standards for training in research are high, the work demanding, and the teacher training program has got to be superimposed on it without serious encroachment. All this underscores the necessity for a *minimum* training program, one which is effective but which is pared down to the practical essentials. The students, we believe, are aware of this effort to include only the most indispensable, and they respect the course for it. Student reaction indicates that the course as a whole is successful, though far from dazzling. A few students catch fire; most accept it without marked enthusiasm, but as something which obviously has relevance (and is required) even if it does not have the intellectual and esthetic fascination of the other courses they are taking. A few—only a few—resist it.

Under such a program, the student, by the second year of graduate work, will have received a respectable amount of background and consequently will be at least minimally prepared to assume teaching responsibilities. These should be limited to a single section of an elementary course, in order to interfere as little as possible with his studies. That he is paid for his services should not confuse the issue, for this teaching assignment should not be considered chiefly a subsidy or scholarship for the student and a source of cheap labor for the university. Both sides should regard it primarily as an introduction to teaching responsibilities, carried on under careful supervision and guidance. Such guidance should be far different from the superficial and inadequate supervision which is normal currently. The supervisor should provide a plan for day-to-day conduct of the course; he should thoroughly discuss the aims of the course with the student-teacher; he should undertake with the student-teacher an analytical examination of textbooks and other materials used; he should provide the student-teacher with guidance in the preparation of tests and examinations; he should provide for the student a planned program of observation of sections parallel to the one the student is teaching; he should visit the student-teacher's classes; and he should hold individual consultations with the student-teacher regarding classroom problems faced by the student-teacher.

In his second year at Harvard, the student is placed in full charge of a section of the elementary course (we do not divide our course into analysis and drill sections). It is most advantageous that he knows intimately what the language philosophy of the department is, is thoroughly familiar with the basic materials, has observed and has studied in some detail the procedures used. To be sure, a major gap exists between knowing how and really being able to, and the actual teaching experience is traumatic, especially at first. But there must be a beginning sometime, and our students are better prepared to begin than most.

Of course, they must be assisted and given further guidance. An experienced teacher is in charge of all sections of the course, and a detailed outline of day-to-day teaching procedures is prepared and supplied to all staff members in the course. There are periodic staff meetings, though these are less frequent than we could wish for maximum effectiveness, a restriction dictated by our "minimum" program. The beginning teacher is encouraged to visit, particularly in the early weeks, a parallel section taught by an experienced teacher. We also encourage intervisiting among the teaching fellows. They in turn are visited by both the head of the course and other experienced teachers. Such visits are always a great psychological strain on the new teacher, and we do all we can to minimize this. Surprise visits are not a part of our program. The teaching fellow is always consulted and the visit arranged for ahead of time. As a result, the teaching fellow prepares carefully for this visit, but we consider this an advantage, rather than the reverse. We want to see them at their best, in order the more confidently to evaluate their abilities and to offer advice. The latter is ordinarily given during a private conference as soon after the visit as possible.

The advice most often found necessary in such conferences through the years has been epitomized and mimeographed. All student-teachers, second- and third-year, as well as first-year teaching fellows, are given a copy of this at the beginning of the year, and urged to refer to it repeatedly. Experience has convinced us that this is one of our most effective teaching aids. It reads as follows:

For All Teaching Fellows

The following Do's and Don't's are a distillation of repeated observation during class visits and subsequent conferences with teaching fellows over a period of years. Please take them very seriously, because every one of them is important. Measure your procedures against them, not casually, but earnestly; not once, but repeatedly, so that the correct technique becomes a habit. You are expected to put all of them into practice.

1. *Don't talk too much.* Give the students a chance.

2. Insist that a student's answer be *distinctly* heard by *every* student *every* time (even though it is only one word).

3. Instantaneous comprehension; split-second response.

4. Books closed *most of the time.* Never let books be used as a crutch.

5. Near-perfect pronunciation. Remember, *you* set the standard. No student can learn to pronounce better than you require him to do.

6. Some choral work *every* hour. Make a personal vow that you will not let a single hour go by without at least fifteen sentences chorally repeated with good intonation at normal speed.

IMPORTANT: the model must always be clear, well pronounced, and with proper intonation.

7. If you get a wrong answer from a student, or if he is unable to give any, get or give the correct answer *fast,* have it repeated by others individually and/or chorally. *Always, always, always* go back to the student who made the mistake or failed to answer and get it from him correctly before you move on.

8. If by chance you call on two students in succession and get wrong answers from both, this is already too much incorrect German. Treat it as an emergency. You must either get the correct answer by calling on someone you know will do it right, or give it at once yourself. Then see (7) above.

9. Don't go on to the next point until you get a response at normal speed and with acceptable intonation.

10. Variety; a single technique will reduce in effectiveness after about 20 minutes.

11. Pattern drill should occupy a substantial portion of each hour.

12. Active attention and participation of *every* student *every* minute. This is your responsibility.

13. Don't repeat. Say it so that they can get it the first time, and then *insist* they do.

14. Pitch level of difficulty so as to elicit only correct answers, but on the threshold of the students' ability. If it's too easy, make it harder; if you get frequent mistakes, this is an *infallible* signal to you to do something else. For whatever reason (students unprepared; poor exercise; too demanding) frequent error in class is your fault, not the students'. Remember Patricia O'Connor's aphorism: "On a test, if the students make too many errors, the students flunk. In classroom drill, if the students make too many errors, the teacher flunks."

15. Keep all the students on their toes all the time, ready for anything. The 50 minutes in the class are their most potent learning time.

16. Teach them something. Don't just find out what they already know. This means drill.

17. Call on people according to your expectation of their ability to give a correct answer. Call on volunteers only occasionally.

18. Don't be satisfied that *one* student can get the right answer (least of all a volunteer). Be sure that all understand and can perform.

19. *Drill* correct answers. Once or twice is not enough. Five times is better. And better still is to ask for variations, changing only one item at a time.

20. Get to *everybody repeatedly every day*.

21. Make split-second decisions constantly. Is it important? Is it worth the time? Is it relevant? Have important skills been ignored?

22. Be *very* sure you know the aims of the course you teach and the general techniques agreed on and frequently check yourself to be sure you are working toward them.

23. All students say (read, speak, repeat) some German sentences every hour.

24. It is good on occasion, when students read from the book, for the teacher to listen without the book to make sure the student is getting across.

25. Don't waste time trying to dig out an answer from a student who doesn't know or isn't prepared.

26. Don't ever do artificial things like changing active to passive or changing sentences into weird tenses and moods or joining two clauses with relative pronouns that result in unnatural utterances.

27. Be sure *all* the students understand what you are driving at.

28. Say it in German!

29. Return tests during the final moments of the class period. Never "go over" the test in class. On hour tests, ask all students getting C or less to make an appointment with you to go over test individually. This appointment need not be longer than 15 to 20 minutes for each student. Let B and A students alone. They don't need your help.

30. Don't solicit isolated questions during class. These are usually a waste of time for everybody but the questioner. If student volunteers one, tell him to see you after class.

31. Give assignments loudly, clearly, prominently, fully. Don't crowd them in at the very end of the period.

And don't forget: there is a total ban on the translation of any sentence, German to English or English to German, from an open book by the student. No exceptions!

Clearly, the implementation of such a program requires far more time than can reasonably be expected of graduate departments and professors. It demands the appointment or designation of a senior member to be in permanent charge. This is not an assignment which can be delegated to younger, temporary, less experienced members of the department, for maturity, specialized knowledge, continuity, and—above all—unquestioned authority are required. The supervisor must obviously be relieved of other departmental responsibilities in order to have time to carry out the program for which he is responsible, yet he must not allow himself to be isolated from the other activities of the department. He must give graduate courses; he must participate in departmental deliberations on scholarly as well as teaching matters; above all, he must publish—he must keep up his scholarly interests. He will be forgiven for being less productive than colleagues who do not have his pedagogical responsibilities, but he will not be forgiven, by colleagues or students, for being nonproductive. Failure on his part to engage in the various non-teaching activities I have mentioned would mean the segmenting of the department's interests into scholarly pursuits on the one hand and pedagogical ones on the other, and a further widening of the gulf which already separates the two. This will be an ever-present danger if programs for the preparation of the teacher are introduced, and there must be constant vigilance to prevent it. If we are to train scholar-teachers, they must be trained by scholar-teachers, not by scholars who are not teachers and teachers who are not scholars. The relevance of each to the other should be constantly implemented.

Since 1958, one of the senior professors in the Harvard German Department has had the additional title of Coordinator of German

Language Courses. A part of his duties is the development of the training program described here and the over-all supervision of the language courses in the department.

If the student has had a teacher-preparation course in his first year and has taught an elementary course in his second year, he should be ready in his third year of graduate study—by which time he will presumably have fulfilled his residence requirements and perhaps be preparing for his general examinations or writing his dissertation—to assume responsibility for two undergraduate sections. One of these should be a section of the same course he has already taught. This would of course reinforce his experience of the previous year. It would also require less of his time, for we all know that one of the not-to-be-underrated joys of teaching is giving a course over again. In addition, his experience should be broadened by teaching an intermediate or advanced course, under supervision and guidance as before, for he is still an apprentice teacher. If, incidentally, the compensation for the three classes taught by the graduate assistant during his second and third years could be evenly divided over the three years of his study, the problem of providing financial aid for the student during his first graduate year without requiring him to teach would perhaps be at least partially solved.

Sometime during this third year, if not before, the student will be expected to take his general examinations. Since under the kind of program which has been outlined he will have been honestly prepared as a teacher as well as a scholar, it is only logical that these examinations reflect this training. They should, therefore, properly include pedagogical as well as scholarly matters. The Proficiency Tests for Teachers and Advanced Students developed by the MLA under contract with the Office of Education[11] could be a valuable device for this purpose, and could also serve as a measure of the effectiveness of the new teaching program.

A graduate teaching program such as this is indeed a minimum program for future college teachers of foreign languages (who, be it remembered, will also be teachers of teachers), yet no program of such an extent is fully implemented in any graduate foreign language department in the entire United States. Many departments are beginning to devote more attention to teaching procedures, however, and the suggestions made here can be considered a reasonable temporary goal. After programs of this nature have been achieved, the profession can perhaps hope that the kind of thorough re-evaluation and revision of all aspects of the undergraduate and graduate programs recommended and documented in the MacAllister report[2] will then become a goal. If and when this occurs, the definition which Robert Louis Stevenson once made of politics—"the only profession for which no preparation is thought necessary"—will no longer be applicable to college foreign language teaching.

References

1. Doctors and masters—good and bad! Report of Standing Committee on Policies in Graduate Education, Assoc. of Graduate Schools, *J. Proceedings and Addresses* (1957).
2. MACALLISTER, ARCHIBALD (May 1964) The preparation of college teachers of modern foreign languages, *PMLA,* **7.**
3. HALL, ROBERT (1960) *Linguistics and Your Language,* 2nd rev. ed. of *Leave Your Language Alone!* Anchor Book A201, Doubleday, New York.
4. GLEASON, HENRY ALLEN (1960) *An Introduction to Descriptive Linguistics,* rev. ed., Holt, New York.
5. HOCKETT, CHARLES FRANCIS (1960) *A Course in Modern Linguistics,* Macmillan, New York.
6. SAPIR, EDWARD (1949) *Language, An Introduction to the Study of Speech,* Harvest Book 7, Harcourt, Brace, New York.
7. MOULTON, WILLIAM G. (1962) *The Sounds of English and German,* Univ. of Chicago Press, Chicago.
8. KUFNER, HERBERT L. (1962) *The Grammatical Structures of English and German,* Univ. of Chicago Press, Chicago. Moulton's and Kufner's books are the first in a series of contrastive structure studies which will describe the similarities and differences between English and French, German, Italian, Russian, and Spanish. The series is under the general editorship of Charles A. Ferguson, Director of the Center for Applied Linguistics, Washington, D.C.
9. *Principles and Methods of Teaching a Second Language,* A Motion Picture Series for Teacher Training: (1) The nature of language and how it is learned, (2) The sounds of language, (3) The organization of language, (4) Words and their meanings, (5) Modern techniques in language teaching. Sponsored and administered by the Modern

Language Association, Center for Applied Linguistics, and Teaching Film Custodians, Inc. Distributed by Teaching Film Custodians, Inc., New York. Each film 16mm; sound; black and white; running time approx. 32 min.

10. PARKER, WILLIAM RILEY (Sept. 1961) *The National Interest and Foreign Languages,* 3rd ed., a discussion guide. Prepared for the U.S. National Commission for UNESCO, Dept. of State Publication 7234. For sale by Supt. of Documents, U.S. Govt. Printing Office, $1.00.

11. *Proficiency Tests for Teachers and Advanced Students,* developed by Modern Language Association, under contract with U.S. Office of Education. Administered by Educational Testing Service, Princeton, N.J. There are seven tests—Speaking, Reading, Writing, Listening Comprehension, Professional Preparation, Applied Linguistics, and Culture—in each of five languages: French, German, Italian, Russian, and Spanish.

CHAPTER IX

Observation of Demonstration Classes as a Method of Teaching Teachers

F. W. NACHTMANN
University of Illinois

THE training of beginning language teachers on the college and university level has been the subject of considerable attention in recent years. Although prospective high school teachers have traditionally received a rather prolonged training in pedagogy, college administrators have too often treated the skills of their profession with implied contempt, assuming that anyone with a degree and a textbook could teach. This situation is changing. As our campuses are thronged with new students, they and their parents and the public at large are less and less satisfied with mediocre instruction. In many universities, graduate assistants now teach most of the elementary classes in foreign languages, as well as in mathematics and English. They are a rather select group, intellectually speaking, and a few are experienced teachers by the time they return to the University for graduate work; but their sheer numbers, their transient status, and the inexperience of many among them have focused attention on the need for a vigorous training program.

In the fall of 1961, the University of Illinois's French Department inaugurated a new system of training its young staff members which has proved practical and expeditious and should be adaptable to most universities and large colleges. It borrowed freely from the practice-teaching system used to train high school teachers and from the observation class technique which has become standard in summer institutes.

Organization of the New Training System

The principal feature of the new system was a demonstration class to be taught by one of the professors and to be attended by all the new teaching assistants added to the staff that year. The conferences on methods which had been held in previous years were retained, but they were made supplementary to the demonstration class. Since the new graduate assistants are regularly assigned to teach the first semester of elementary French, one of the 8 o'clock sections of this course was chosen as the demonstration class, and all of the new assistants were assigned to teach other sections meeting later in the day. The schedule of daily lesson assignments was arranged so that even though the morning and afternoon classes did not meet on the same sequence, none of the participants would teach a given assignment before seeing it demonstrated. They were not required to make any preparation in their own time. They were expected to make out a lesson plan while observing the 8 o'clock section, to take any necessary notes on the techniques, and to apply the same method in their own sections, distributing their time among the various activities as the master teacher had done. Although any large classroom would have been adequate, the experiment was favored by the availability of a classroom with a concealed observation gallery equipped with a one-way glass stretching most of the length of one wall, the ends being completed by screen wire which let the sound come through. The floor of the observation gallery was about 3 feet above the level of the classroom floor and gave a very adequate view of both teacher and students from the side.

The undergraduates in the observation class were a completely random selection. It was desired that the trainees see how the teacher would handle all types of students. The latter were not told at first that there was anything special about their class. Some of them did not know for several days that they were being observed, and when they found out it seemed to make no difference.

The senior staff member who served as the master teacher was a person of considerable experience on both the high school and university level and with a keen interest in efficient teaching. He was not the chairman of the course, but naturally it would be quite possible to combine the two positions. In this case, the chairman, who was also a senior staff member teaching one section of the elementary course, was left more free for his administrative responsibilities, and he also assumed the major share of the follow-up visits to the assistants' classes.

Thirteen new graduate assistants were assigned to the training program; two other graduate students attended on a voluntary basis; the chairman of the elementary courses was usually present; and there were occasional visitors. The thirteen assigned participants were not as a group complete novices in their profession. As for their linguistic background, three were native French speakers, and of the others all but three had studied in France for a period of from three months to two years. From the standpoint of academic background, three held M.A.s, seven had A.B.s (in most cases with additional credits) and three held French or Belgian degrees. All but two had had a teaching methods course or teaching experience. Five had taught in American high schools; four had taught in American colleges; and five had taught English or French in European schools. Several of them combined these different kinds of teaching experience.

A demonstration class needs, of course, a regular conference time between the master teacher and his observers in order to take stock and to establish guidelines for the future. Meetings were held as in previous years, but now there was something definite and concrete to discuss. Since the demonstration class met four times a week, Tuesday through Friday, the weekly seminar for the observers was scheduled for Monday at 10 o'clock. The chairman of the elementary courses presided, assisted by the demonstration teacher. The latter would comment upon and promote discussion of the techniques he was using with the undergraduates. In addition, this meeting was the occasion for discussion of matters which do not lend themselves to demonstration, such as methods and standards of grading and the defining of the responsibilities of the monitor in the language laboratory, where each assistant was assigned to spend one hour a week. The chairman of the course also used the Monday meeting to dispose of administrative matters such as settling registration problems and appointing examination committees.

One of the features of this training program borrowed from the practice teaching courses and from many of the observation class arrangements was the direct participation of the observers. After some three weeks of observation, the graduate assistants were invited to take a turn teaching the demonstration class while the senior teacher retired to the observation gallery. Their appearance before the class was facilitated by the fact that they already knew the names, personalities and abilities of the students, whom they had been observing for weeks from the gallery. Each assistant taught the class for one day, and from the date that the observers began to participate in the instruction, the class was usually handled two days of the week by assistants. The one designated to take the class had an individual conference with the regular teacher in advance to work out the lesson plan.

The undergraduates in the demonstration class were prepared for this new phase by the master teacher who explained to them that he reserved for himself the entire responsibility for giving them a grade in the course and that he would always be present in the observation gallery even when not teaching the class. He added a little flattery about the importance to the program of this special class. He built up the reputation of the graduate assistants in advance of their appearance by emphasizing their knowledge of the French language and France, by explaining that many of them were experienced teachers who were simply being trained to "do things our way", and that in all cases they were actually teaching other sections of this same course at other hours of the day. He also pointed out that the students were having an opportunity to get acquainted in advance with some of their future French instructors. After the graduate assistants began to participate in the teaching, the

Monday conference served also as a time for a critique of their performance, both by the master teacher and by their colleagues.

The obligatory attendance at the demonstration class ended on December 1, but the Monday conferences continued through to the end of the semester, being reduced however to a bimonthly meeting during December and January. Administratively, this weekly seminar on methods plus the obligatory attendance at the observation class constituted a non-credit graduate course, French 405: "Teaching College French".

The most important reason for the choice of this training program was the need for an expeditious means of getting the annual new group of teachers launched. Having meetings and simply lecturing to a group of young newcomers about what one wants them to do has been found to be ineffectual; a visit to their classes later often reveals that they did not understand at all and are doing something quite different from what was desired. A two-semester period of training and observation before turning the graduate assistant loose with his own class, such as that proposed by Stein of Harvard (*PMLA*, May 1961) would appear to be excellent, but who has that much time and money? The French Department of the University of Illinois adds from ten to fifteen graduate assistants to its staff each year, and from these the teachers of the elementary courses have to be drawn immediately. By showing them the precise subject matter of the day's lesson being presented to a class by a competent teacher just in advance of their own teaching, it was possible to get good instruction into the classroom immediately.

The weekly seminar on methods is, of course, a very necessary part of the demonstration class procedure. Unlike the usual methods course, however, in which the student complains all too often that he gets only theory, here it was possible to refer to what the participant had *seen* and to explain the reasons for it. Moreover, the graduate assistants were able to contribute to the discussion from their experience in applying the demonstration techniques in their own classes. Often the discussion was quite lively and there was an occasional clash of opinions. Sometimes the demonstration teacher discussed in advance the techniques which he expected to employ in class during the coming weeks. Not infrequently also, he drove a point home by using the graduate assistants themselves as a beginning French class.

The training program was not only expeditious from the French Department's standpoint; it was economical of the participants' time. Any conscientious beginning teacher in a school has to spend hours every week getting acquainted with the new textbook and making lesson plans. In this case, these activities were achieved during the observation class with scarcely any extra expenditure of time. Moreover, the results were far richer than they would have been if the graduate assistants had worked alone. The participants were encouraged to plagiarize freely, using in their own classes later in the day any of the master teacher's illustrations, drills or special devices which struck them as effective. A great difference between instruction by a beginner in the profession, even a talented beginner, and instruction by a teacher of many years' experience is the many tricks of the trade that the latter has learned and uses in putting his subject across. Here even the observers without imagination were handed the whole thing on a platter.

The participation of the observers in the teaching of the demonstration class proved to be a very useful aspect of the procedure. The knowledge that each one would eventually have to get up and display his wares before his colleagues kept him more tensely attentive to what was going on. As a matter of fact, the assistants showed great interest in just how each of their colleagues handled the demonstration class. It would have been desirable to give the graduate assistants more than one opportunity to teach in public, but the large number of participants in the program made it necessary to limit them to a single performance. This is much less opportunity to participate than the high school practice teacher would have, but, on the other hand, all the graduate assistants had their own sections in which, later in the day, they could apply what they had learned to their own students. Another reason for limiting the substitute teachers to just two days a week was in order not to deprive them for too long of the opportunity to observe the master teacher.

Success of the Course

There were a number of indications that the demonstration-class training program was succeeding very well. One month after the beginning of the semester, the chairman of the course reported that not one of the participating assistants had been in to see him individually with a problem. In previous years the first weeks of class had brought a rather steady stream of visitors asking for advice on their teaching problems. Another indication of the effectiveness of the system was provided by a visit, a few days after the semester started, to the class of one of the assistants who had had no previous teaching experience or training. She was found to be giving a very good imitation of an experienced teacher, faithfully putting into practice the techniques she had seen applied in the observation class that morning. When the assistants themselves took over the demonstration class, they all gave good performances, and most of them gave excellent ones. Follow-up visits to the assistants' classes indicated that all of those who participated in this methods course were able to incorporate into their own teaching most of what they saw. There were individual variations, as is natural.

One of the greatest services of the demonstration class was that of standardization of procedure, which is probably more important than the instruction of beginners. In any language department it is important to have an understanding as to what skills are to be emphasized and what techniques are to be used in the elementary and intermediate classes. In a large language department of which the teaching staff of the first semester course alone may number twenty people, the task is decidedly challenging. The group of new graduate assistants always includes a considerable number with teacher training or teaching experience, but they come from all parts of the country, from foreign countries, and from quite varied backgrounds. In order to function as part of a consistent program in which their students are exposed to the same method, they need some kind of strong integrating influence. Actually, if the public were more perceptive, it would see that the faults it finds with the teaching done by graduate assistants are due not so much to the lack of talent on their part as to the failure of their superiors to organize and supervise, to present clear goals and a definite philosophy, and to demand efficiency.

The need for demonstration is even greater when the audio-lingual method is being emphasized. Many teachers have not themselves been trained through such a method and have no idea how to proceed. An inexperienced teacher, for instance, usually has little idea how to use the choral technique. He does not realize how much oral repetition is necessary on the part of the teacher and how much has to be required of the students in an elementary class. He needs to be shown that it is entirely possible to demand and receive something other than inaudible, halting responses. This insistence on excellence is something much easier to demonstrate than to describe. The technique by which an experienced, successful teacher drives ahead cheerfully and vigorously, always keeping the pressure on every member of the class to perform according to the best of his ability, is something which needs to be seen; it cannot be imparted well through description.

The new training system retained from the older procedures the inspection of the performance of graduate assistants while they were teaching their own sections. Visits to neophytes by their seniors cannot be neglected until the new personalities become known, predictable quantities to their superiors on the teaching staff. Even after repeated demonstrations, some instructors needed to be prodded to apply all that they had seen. However, in all cases where the graduate assistants who participated in this training program were visited in their own sections they were found to be doing at least a satisfactory job, and very often an excellent one. Where it was necessary to suggest changes to them, it was possible to remind them of something which they had *seen*. That old excuse, "Oh, I thought you meant . . ." had now become irrelevant. Everybody knew exactly what was meant.

Conclusions

The success of the French Department's practical training program for its new teaching assistants brought quick imitation by other language departments. The program has been continued essentially in its original form, but the master teacher for subsequent semesters has been chosen from among the senior graduate assistants. Among the dozens available, there are always two or three of mature experience and outstanding ability. Another witness to the success and prestige of the experiment is that the foreign language departments have now acquired their own special demonstration classroom. The first observation class was held in a neighboring building in a classroom assigned to the English Department, which had inherited it from the Child Development Laboratory, once held in that building. Now a new demonstration classroom has been constructed in the building which houses the modern language departments, and the room is shared equally by the four major departments concerned. The concealed observation gallery has a seating capacity limited to fifteen; therefore, it is necessary to run the training program for the French Department, with its large number of annual recruits, on a two-session basis—one at 8 a.m. and another at 1 p.m. Besides serving its principal purpose, this special classroom has served as a convenient facility to permit various people to enter the classroom situation unobtrusively for purposes of observation, visiting or training.

The participants in the program were cooperative and seemed appreciative that the guidance was made practical and explicit. Most young teachers are eager for suggestions, and are usually anxious to conform to the established policy if they know what it is. Demonstration classes are not new, but this particular system has the practical advantage that each observer may apply immediately in his own class what he has just seen demonstrated. In the weekly conferences with the master teacher and the chairman of the course, it is possible to refer to practical situations familiar to everyone. Thus the observation class arrangement serves to provide a technique for those who need one, to improve techniques for those who need improvement, and to standardize procedures for all. It is remarkably well adapted to the needs of a large university.

CHAPTER X

A Model Design for the In-service Training of Foreign Language Teachers

DAVID M. FELDMAN

California State College, Fullerton, California

PERHAPS at no other time in the history of the profession has there been expressed by the nation's secondary school teachers of modern foreign languages such widespread recognition of the need for in-service training programs designed to keep the teacher abreast of the rapidly developing technological and methodological advances in the field. Paradoxically, although both teachers and administrators enthusiastically support the wide variety of federally and locally supported in-service programs currently available, they have been quick to voice serious dissatisfaction with many features of existing programs and, in some cases, to point out that many in-service training opportunities are not quite as "available" as they appear to be.

As part of a project under contract with the Language Development Section of the U.S. Office of Education (Feldman, 1963a), a broad and varied population of secondary school language teachers, supervisors, and administrators was queried to determine the reasons for their dissatisfaction with current in-service offerings and to cull suggestions for eventual improvement. The results of one survey show that it is necessary to re-evaluate current in-service programs in the light of three major questions:

1. How realistically can the term "in-service" be applied to many of the programs currently being offered to teachers?

2. What kinds of educational experiences actually lend themselves to the in-service format?

3. To what extent can the *experienced* language teacher really find intellectual stimulation, as well as information, in available in-service programs?

A majority of those responding to the questionnaire suggested that the "in-service" concept was, from the secondary school teacher's point of view, often too unrealistically interpreted. An example of this was the custom of calling programs offered on weekends and particularly during the longer vacation periods "in-service". Teachers felt that the term was euphemistic in this context, especially when the programs interfere with financial, family, or community responsibilities scheduled for these periods. Objections were also raised to programs and activities accessible only on a released-time basis when not all, and often not even many, interested teachers were able to arrange for such released time. Teachers in outlying districts were also quick to add that the cost involved in traveling often as much as 150 miles in each direction, and in some cases staying overnight, to participate in the nearest in-service programs in their states often made participation impossible.

University extension programs with late afternoon or evening courses have gone far toward reaching the geographically distant teacher, but teachers in both rural districts and large cities maintained that such extension courses often fail to place the particular needs of the post-graduate, experienced teacher in the center of the course plan.

Although considerable and enthusiastic praise was understandably lavished upon the more extensive curricula, such as academic-year and summer NDEA institutes, academic year or summer study abroad, and exchange teacher plans, it is only by strained analogy, those questioned felt, that such offerings might reasonably be called "in-service". In these larger programs there is also the problem that of the many who apply, only a few can be accepted.

Improving In-service Programs

We cannot but be struck by the potent unanimity of opinion concerning the divergence between what in-service programs have been and what the responding teachers and others have indicated these programs should be. Since in-service programs are designed for these very teachers and supervisors, their concept of what "in-service" means must be considered fundamental, even if that implies revisions in the traditional in-service training.

The second major area of concern was the apparent inappropriateness of the format of many of the in-service courses and workshops presented and, by implication, the apparent irrelevance of much of what was offered to the particular educational needs that the programs were designed to fulfill. It was suggested that "pep talks", demonstrations such as "teaching the contrast between the Spanish imperfect and preterite with toy trains", and reminiscences of a local administrator's informal tour through several French schools are hardly the most appropriate material for in-service courses. Indeed, most respondents agreed that the all-too-frequent in-service offering made up of "one shot" lectures, demonstrations, or "cultural" talks, with the occasional workshop—which is frequently no more than a combination of the above—no more serves a well-designed, intellectually sound program than *hors d'oeuvres* and dessert replace a balanced meal. The error is by no means always on the side of superficiality, however. The universities frequently insist, even in late-afternoon and evening programs, on depth of detail not really needed by the high school language teacher. Such experience often discourages him from voluntary participation in other in-service programs. It is not that the language teacher is no longer interested in the dawn of the epic, for example, but rather that such interests are perhaps better pursued in a summer or a year devoted to enrichment studies in collateral areas. The teachers' in-service needs, on the contrary, lie in a far more practical, yet no less significant, area.

The third area of dissatisfaction involves the frequent lack of intellectual stimulation for the *experienced* teacher. His needs are understandably different from those of the apprentice. Assuming he has a reasonable command of the language he is speaking and a sincere desire for self-improvement, he feels offended by the "lecture" approach in his in-service experiences. He seeks, rather, an opportunity to synthesize his knowledge, experience, and insights, on the one hand, and new information, techniques, and attitudes on the other. His professional pride rebels somewhat against the more-or-less uncompromising "one-way" nature of the lecture course. Yet the lecture course is frequently the only opportunity open and available to him.

Given these reasonable objections, a set of requirements emerges, *sine quibus non,* we might say, for truly effective in-service programs. The principal requirements are:

1. In-service programs must be made available during the regular school term at hours and in locations accessible to all teachers in the district, without need either for released time or reimbursement for travel expenses.

2. The course(s) offered must be directly relevant to the teacher's classroom duties and must be planned with his needs uppermost in mind.

3. The course(s) must make use of instructional techniques by means of which the experienced teacher will be able to synthesize his own training and professional capabilities with the new information and techniques he is learning. The teacher will then be able to use his own classroom as a laboratory in which he may refine his discoveries by applying them and evaluate new theories and techniques immediately after encountering them.

Colorado Pilot Project

Developing a program of in-service training that will fully meet the needs of every teacher under all the circumstances just outlined is a nearly impossible task. It is not difficult, however, to improve upon what has traditionally been done. The following plan*, on

* A project carried to completion at the University of Colorado, 1962–64.

which the author worked, has proved its effectiveness in moving toward fulfillment of these prerequisites and is presented here as a model design on which improved versions may be based. It is adaptable to a variety of subject matter and field conditions.

The relevance of the course to the teacher's immediate professional needs was the first of three primary concerns. Experience in the NDEA summer language institutes had indicated (Feldman, 1964) that a majority of participating teachers found the potentially most important and useful, and yet most difficult to grasp, material to be the application of the findings of linguistic analysis to the teaching of one or more foreign languages. Once teachers are introduced to this material, their desire for further self-training in their control of the language (conversation, composition, etc.) and in their understanding of the cultural background of the peoples who speak the language arises naturally from, and is most highly stimulated by, the increased awareness that such control and understanding are necessary to take full advantage of the new approaches to language teaching (Feldman and Schindler, 1964). Applied linguistics, then, was to be the subject matter of the course.

The second of the primary concerns was to make the program available to all teachers in the selected districts* without need for either released time or travel reimbursement. Groups of teachers would meet in their own districts at a location and time convenient to all, to study recent views of the nature of language and of how it is most efficiently learned and taught. Together they would examine new teaching materials, audio-visual aids, and equipment now available, evaluate them, and share various ways of using them to greatest advantage. To overcome the negative influence of the lecture-classroom approach and to liberate the program from dependence upon the availability locally of competent instructors, it was decided to use a modification (Schindler and Feldman, 1963) of the independent group study technique (Leuba, 1963). In this project, the director met a total of only three times with the participants in each location once the instructional program had begun.

* Colorado Springs and Thornton, Colorado.

The third concern was for teaching materials adequate to the purpose. A set of materials had to be designed to acquaint teachers with the application of descriptive linguistics to language pedagogy and with the main currents of the audio-lingual approach. At the same time, it was necessary to provide a carefully selected collection of reference books, tapes, and films which the participants could peruse and use voluntarily for their own self-improvement. This step was essential if the program were to be truly effective in outlying districts where the teachers could not be expected to have access to extensive library facilities. The final version of the text (Feldman, 1963b) consists of twelve lessons, an extensive annotated bibliography, discussion questions, and directions for the use of the secondary source collection. A separate binding contains specific instructions on the nature of the independent group study program. This creates a completely portable and fully exportable package. Arrangements were made to grant participants graduate credit at the University of Colorado upon successful completion of the course. Administrative details were handled by the university's extension division. The hope here was that for once the technique of instruction would match the need and the material. Given the course materials, all that is necessary is the desire of the group of teachers to learn. No professor is needed.

There are three possible types of leadership that an independent group study program might employ. The least successful is the permanent leader. If a group selects a permanent leader, it is necessary to insure that the leader's qualifications rest more on his experience with and skill in effective discussion leading than on substantive superiority. The "image" of the permanent discussion leader is of the greatest importance. If his appointment is made because of his greater knowledgeability or experience in the areas taught, it will be difficult, if not impossible, for him to rid himself of the "teacher" role and help the group become self-sufficient enough to evolve its own answers. The second and third possibilities are of the shared leadership type. One such arrangement makes everyone responsible for the group's progress, rather than setting one individual apart and assigning the responsibility to him. Each participant thus gains a feeling of personal commitment to the group. In the peculiar psychology of teaching teachers, the absence of an "authority" figure is interpreted among mature groups as a testimony of faith in their ability to work productively together. The other shared leadership plan calls for a rotating moderator. This is based on the same principle as the simple shared leadership plan, yet differs from it in that a single individual assumes responsibility for insuring that everyone who wishes to be given the opportunity to contribute. The moderator curbs the overly vocal and draws out the reticent.

For the practical application of the course content to the teaching situation, the study guide represents an even balance between the principles of descriptive linguistics and the practical application of them in the classroom. The twelve chapters of the study guide prepared for this project were:

1. The development of the audio-lingual technique.
2. Descriptive linguistics and language teaching.
3. A linguistic teaching procedure.
4. Significant contrasts and the teaching of pronunciation.
5. Tagmemics and syntactic drills.
6. The language laboratory.
7. Reading and writing in the audio-lingual approach.
8. Testing and evaluation.
9. Selecting and adapting audio-lingual textbooks.
10. "Culture" in the audio-lingual approach.
11. Planning four-, six-, and eight-year sequences.
12. Inferring meaning and building vocabulary.

It is impossible, of course, to measure accurately the total progress of project participants with regard to their attitudes, receptivity to new materials and techniques, application of course materials in their classrooms, and so forth. It is possible, however, to gain a partial insight into their relative progress by means of examination. For purposes of the project, the MLA Proficiency Tests in applied linguistics and professional preparation were administered at the beginning and again at the end of the project.

By comparing these results with those of the 1962 NDEA Summer Institute participants, we should gain some insight into their relative improvement. In comparing these figures, it must be remembered that no selective process was used in choosing project participants and that the total course meeting time was approximately 30 hours, compared to an average minimum of approximately 40 hours in most summer institutes, and that no time was taken from the participants' normal full-time teaching schedules.

MEAN CONVERTED SCORES

| | 1962 NDEA Summer Institutes || Colorado Pilot Project ||
	Applied linguistics	Professional preparation	Applied linguistics	Professional preparation
Pre-test	43.667	59.306	43.545	62.400
Post-test	49.586	67.043	46.818	66.091

NUMBER OF PARTICIPANTS IN PERCENTILE RANK, GENERALIZED IN 10% GRADES
COLORADO PILOT PROJECT

| Percentile rank | Applied linguistics || Professional preparation ||
	Pre-tests	Post-tests	Pre-tests	Post-tests
90–100	2	2	4	4
80–89	–	8	2	2
70–79	2	2	–	6
60–69	2	2	6	6
50–59	4	4	2	4
40–49	–	–	2	–
30–39	8	–	6	–
20–29	2	2	–	–
10–19	2	2	–	–
0–9	–	–	–	–
Average	30–39	70–79	60–69	70–79

Number of Participants Changing Percentile Rank
Colorado Pilot Project

No. of percentiles	Applied linguistics	Professional preparation
5	4	–
4	4	2
3	2	4
2	2	6
1	4	6
0	2	4
−1	–	–
−2	2	–
−3	2	–

Number of Participants Rising from Lower Half of Percentile
Ranking to Upper Half
Colorado Pilot Project

	Applied linguistics	Professional preparation
Began in lower half	12 out of 22	8 out of 22
Began in upper half	10 out of 22	14 out of 22
Rose from lower to upper half	8 out of 12	8 out of 8
Total in upper half at end of course	18 out of 22	22 out of 22

This final table is significant because, compared with national institute means, half of the pilot group began in the lower 50% of the tested teachers in the nation. At the end of the project, all participants rose to at least the upper 50% in professional preparation, and 92% rose to the upper half in applied linguistics.

Conclusions

The Colorado pilot in-service program was demonstrably practical, efficient to a high degree, and flexible. It showed that such a program must maintain from the very beginning an atmosphere of open frankness in which each participant expects to learn from his fellows as well as from the material. Each participant should realize that his professional problems are shared with each and every colleague and that each participant's desire to improve the quality of his own professionalism depends upon his ability to appreciate the mutuality of the problems he is facing. Only a program based upon a recognition of this ground principle has real hopes of success. Finally, this approach to the problem of in-service education develops within the participant an attitude of open-mindedness and pride in the rapid development of his profession and in the principles behind its development.

References

FELDMAN, DAVID M. (1963a) *Elaboration and Experimental Evaluation of Procedures and Specialized Materials for In-Service Training of Secondary School Teachers of Modern Foreign Languages*, U.S. Office of Education, Washington, D.C.

FELDMAN, DAVID M. (1963b) *The Modern Teaching of Spanish*, U.S. Office of Education, Washington, D.C.

FELDMAN, DAVID M. (1964) *The National Defense Summer Language Institute for Secondary School Teachers of German at the University of Colorado—Report of the Director*, U.S. Office of Education, Washington, D.C.

FELDMAN, DAVID M., and SCHINDLER, BARBARA (1964) An in-service alternative to the summer institute program, *Modern Language J.*, **48**, No. 2, 88–91.

LEUBA, CLARENCE (1963) *Using Groups in Independent Study*, Antioch College Reports, No. 5, Yellow Springs, Ohio.

SCHINDLER, BARBARA, and FELDMAN, DAVID M. (1963) The application of discussion methods to foreign language teaching, *Colorado Speech J.*, **5**, No. 1, 7–10.

CHAPTER XI

Continuum in Language Learning

Everett V. O'Rourke
California State Department of Education

In the near future, competency in foreign language should be as prevalent in the United States as it is in countries that have common geographical borders across which people and languages move freely. Competency in any foreign language can be acquired in the schools if, among other factors, a consistent, not varied, continuum of learning (articulation) is established and maintained.

Articulation must pervade all levels. For some languages, it will begin in the elementary school and continue through the junior college and university. Students of language have a right to expect the instructional process and the curriculum to be planned and executed so that progress from level to level will be achieved smoothly and not in spite of a series of obstacles.

If there is to be continuity, the teachers must be competent, the method of instruction must be consistent throughout, the materials of instruction and the resources for learning must be proper and adequate, the short-term and long-term goals must be attainable, and the techniques and instruments of evaluation must be such that they truly evaluate and test both the learner and the program of learning. But in the long run, it is the continuing unvaried program that produces competence in the language student.

There are competent teachers who understand and teach by the audio-lingual approach and there are those who are familiar with the grammar-reading-translation method and feel that it is the best. An increasing trend in many schools and colleges in the last several years has been to instruct in accordance with the audio-lingual approach. Outstanding professional and governmental organizations advocate the newer methodology. Foreign language institutes and workshops have been training teachers to understand and use the new method and to have full control of the language being taught. Given adequate time, all schools will have teachers who have had this training. But can the students wait? Should they be caught in the middle while the schools shift gears? Should a teacher in one grade forgo the audio-lingual approach because a few teachers in the next grade cling to the reading-grammar-translation method? But this is being done! Teachers in many instances are saying, "I cannot teach the way I would like to because other teachers in this school refuse to change." Furthermore, some high school teachers' methods are being affected because some college and university foreign language instructors insist on placing students on the basis of their abilities to read and to translate, rather than on their competencies in listening comprehension, speaking, reading, and writing. However, a change is slowly coming about in colleges and universities as well as in the high schools and elementary schools.

Materials of instruction and resources for learning present a similar problem. Although outside the scope of this paper, the question must be asked: Can teaching materials designed for use with the one method be transformed for use with the other, or must new materials be developed?

What is being done about the obstacles to a smooth continuum in foreign language curriculum and instruction? While many worthwhile programs of articulation are being developed in other states, the author of this paper is familiar with educational procedures and plans for articulation between levels and between districts, counties, colleges, and universities in California, and will cite them here to illustrate what can be done.

The Foreign Language Liaison Committee

Quadrilateral cooperative articulation planning appears in the work of the Foreign Language Liaison Committee of the California

Articulation Conference. The Articulation Conference, which has been in operation for about thirty years, is made up of representatives from the secondary schools, the junior colleges, the State Colleges and the University of California. One of its main tasks has been the discussion of the programs of learning at the various levels and to assist in establishing and maintaining smooth transition and transfer of students, insofar as possible, from one level of learning to the next. From time to time the Articulation Conference requests that a specific study be made in a given academic field to explore the problems and issues and make recommendations for the improvement of articulation or continuum of learning.

Early in 1963 the Articulation Conference requested that each of the four segments making up the Conference appoint six people to study and investigate the whole range of problems related to articulation in foreign language instruction in California. These twenty-four people, designated as the Liaison Committee on Foreign Languages, held their first meeting in March 1963. The Committee proceeded to explore the dimensions of the many problems. None of them appeared to have easy and ready solutions.

The Committee members identified six major issues and appointed a subcommittee to investigate each and to prepare a report. On each of the six subcommittees there were representatives from each of the segments that constitute the Conference.

Subcommittee No. 1 was directed to study the instructional objectives and articulation points in foreign language programs. It was felt that any system of continuum of learning would have to be based on clearly defined objectives for the different levels of the program.

Subcommittee No. 2 was given the task of investigating the meaning and implications of the terms "lower division" and "upper division" courses in foreign language programs. This issue involves the junior colleges in California as well as the colleges and universities in view of the fact that many high schools are scheduling longer sequences of language learning.

Subcommittee No. 3 undertook to explore college placement for students who wish to continue working in the language they studied in high school. Involved in this problem is the possible equivalency between the high school language courses and the lower division college language courses, the question of granting credit at the college level for courses taken in high school, and the measurement of each student's level of achievement in the several skills in the language.

Subcommittee No. 4 was assigned to examine the foreign language teacher education programs. It was agreed by the Liaison Committee that without certain basic, common standards of pedagogical approach and effectiveness of instruction any attempt to articulate the levels of instruction might be difficult to attain.

Subcommittee No. 5 agreed to design a method of collecting and disseminating information on practices, plans and policies adopted by various institutions at all levels of language instruction. It was stated that accurate and current comprehensive, pertinent information would be necessary to assist each institution to maintain articulation with others.

Subcommittee No. 6 was created to determine whether, in California at a certain school level, there is a tendency to stress one foreign language to the exclusion of others. If this were true, some felt, the articulation of multilanguages in California schools would be aggravated if not deterred.

Thirteen months after the initial meeting of the Liaison Committee, tentative general agreements were summarized at the Articulation Conference meeting approximately as follows.

1. The ultimate objective of any complete foreign language program should be: a reasonable mastery of the language, including the four skills—listening, speaking, reading, writing; knowledge of the literary masterpieces in that language; insights into the culture of the people who use the language and its writing system; and, if the student is planning to teach the language, the ability to analyze the language and to use effective pedagogical methods. Each level of language teaching should be an effective step toward achievement of these goals.

In planning language curricula it is important to establish, for all four language skills, levels of proficiency which can be measured by nationally validated tests, not by semester or by quarter units devised locally. Efforts must be made to try such tests until they prove to be acceptable and reliable yardsticks for student achievement and placement, language qualification, and teacher accreditation.

2. Collection, compilation and dissemination of information and data on foreign language programs and their operation should be continued, and funds should be made available for this purpose. Such communication is essential for the development and maintenance of properly articulated foreign language programs from the beginning level through the final level in schools and colleges, and will help to foster uniformity and excellence of language programs.

The Liaison Committee feels that its job is only partially done. There is a need for permanent coordinating committees and committees for each language taught in the schools and colleges in the state. The Articulation Conference has agreed that the Committee should continue its work and representatives from elementary schools will be added to it. The Committee will continue to meet and reports made by the Committee to the Conference will be given wide publicity throughout the state.

The Foreign Language Curriculum Subcommittee

The Foreign Language Curriculum Subcommittee of the California Association of Secondary School Administrators is responsible for another statewide program of data collection and for increased activity in establishing and maintaining articulation of foreign language curriculum and instruction. Through interviews and questionnaires, data and information were gathered from a limited and select number of secondary schools concerning: their own instructional programs as well as those of their "feeder" schools; the placement of students arriving from "feeder" schools, from other districts, and from within the district; tests used for achievement and placement; the grouping of students within the programs;

scheduling; steps taken to insure continuity of the program of instruction; teacher preparation and inservice training; and the most valuable practices used to attain continuity.

This was not definitive study. Districts having varied organizations such as 6–3–3, 6–2–4, and 8–4, unified or union, were questionnaired and interviewed. The results were offered as guidelines for county, district, and school personnel interested in a continuum of foreign language study.

The findings indicated trends, problems and solutions, in general, as follows: Some of the districts, less than half of those interviewed, were using the audio-lingual approach; most of the districts were employing the audio-lingual approach in beginning courses with plans to expand this methodology into intermediate and advanced courses; the selection, adoption, and use of instructional materials showed consistency and careful coordination between many high schools and their "feeder" schools.

Student placement at each succeeding level or grade is on the basis of one or more of the following criteria: teacher recommendations; a grade earned (nonspecified); a C grade or better; or, in a very few schools, test scores plus teacher recommendations. Placement in an audio-lingual class of a transfer student who has been studying under a traditional method, or in a traditional class of a transfer student who has been studying under the audio-lingual method, presents problems, the degree of difficulty depending on the teaching, grouping, and guidance practices of the receiving district. The majority of the districts that are not now using grouping practices in foreign languages stated that they are planning to do so in the near future.

Many districts attempting to partially solve the articulation problem by having all teachers instruct according to one method are using the following techniques and in-service programs: vertical curriculum committees, workshops, NDEA institutes, staff meetings, extension courses, special in-service classes run by the district, demonstrations, visitations, textual material, recruitment, consultants from outside the district, laboratory briefing, and NDEA projects.

All the schools and districts interviewed and questioned provide some means of maintaining a continuum of learning. Following are some of the practices:

1. "Articulation" meetings, which most of the districts considered among the most valuable practices used. Regularly scheduled meetings of the teachers and administrators of all three levels of school organization in unified and nonunified districts, vertical curriculum meetings and interdistrict curriculum meetings, and group meetings within each language have provided schools with the most effective means of solving problems and attaining continuity.

2. County-wide groups working on foreign language curricula, instruction and articulation.

3. Meetings that bring together administrators, curriculum consultants and directors, foreign language department heads and foreign language teachers from high schools and elementary schools with a special foreign language consultant from outside the district, with a member of a county staff, or with a consultant from the State Department of Education.

4. Meetings at which the head of the language department in the high school coordinates the work of high school language teachers with elementary school administrators and teachers.

5. Meetings of teaching, curriculum, and administrative staff.

6. Meetings of administrators, supervisors, and special teachers with a consultant from the State Department of Education, followed by meetings with other special language consultants from outside the district, and by in-district meetings of administrators, curriculum consultants, foreign language teachers, and department heads in elementary and secondary schools.

7. Meetings of high school and elementary principals and teachers and head counselor from the high school.

8. Meetings of elementary and secondary school foreign language teachers with district curriculum coordinator.

9. Original planning by curriculum representatives from elementary and high school districts, followed by meetings with foreign language coordinators, principals, and teachers.

10. Commercial or locally developed courses of study uniformly adopted to insure that students will be exposed to the same methods, materials, and testing, and that they will cover the same ground. In several cases, the study guides call for an early review of the material previously covered, in an effort to assure continuity.

11. Placement examinations in situations where teachers are not equally prepared in the audio-lingual method, and where students come from a variety of programs with a variety of approaches.

A Unified School District

The Plumas Unified School District of five elementary schools, five multigraded elementary schools and four junior–senior high schools in the California Sierra reported as follows on planning and achieving an articulated foreign language program:

In 1963, the administrators and teachers in this unified district established a program of foreign language instruction in Grades 6, 7 and 8, which would meet the State of California legal requirements and, at the same time, coordinate and provide proper language background for the already instituted college preparatory foreign language program in Grades 9–12 inclusive.

These administrators and teachers decided that it was necessary to find sources of help and guidance. They discovered that:

1. The California State Department of Education in general and the Bureaus of Elementary and Secondary Education in particular are good and valuable sources of both inspiration and concrete suggestions.

2. The National Defense Education Act, under provisions of Title III B, Consultant Service, provide help with workshops and expert leadership in foreign language curriculum building.

3. Summer and year-long foreign language institutes offer opportunities for teachers to up-grade and reinforce foreign language instructional skills.

4. The Modern Language Association of America, the Foreign Language Association of Northern California and several other

professional organizations in this area are rich sources of information and help.

5. Discussion of foreign language programs with administrators and teachers in other districts, already involved in early foreign language instruction, would be valuable.

6. Several foreign language curriculum and instructional guides from other districts and states would be useful.

If they were to be successful in implementing this program, they would have to emphasize cooperation between educational levels and instill enthusiasm for the program.

One of the first moves was to invite a consultant from the California State Department of Education to a meeting with all principals and district administrators on March 15, 1962. The consultant gave the background of the California legislation, told about activities of some districts in California which have set up elementary school foreign language programs and expanded secondary school programs, and discussed the following problems: finding qualified teachers; educating all students in Grades 6, 7 and 8 in a foreign language or in foreign languages; new methods in foreign language teaching; minimal equipment for the foreign language classroom; testing and texts for foreign language instruction at the elementary and secondary levels; ways and means of articulating the foreign language programs; and other pertinent items.

During the school year 1962–63, consultants were brought to the district under the auspices of the National Defense Education Act, Title III B, for two workshops in which all the foreign language teachers in the district, selected teachers in the elementary schools, district office administrators and all principals and teachers for the five multigraded schools participated. The consultants gave demonstrations of the audio-lingual approach to foreign language instruction, gave talks on instructional techniques, offered suggestions for setting up a foreign language program in the elementary schools which would articulate with the secondary school program, and showed various kinds of texts and instructional materials.

From the workshops, supplemented by other district and individual school meetings, emanated a streamlined course of study for Grades

6–8 which attempts to articulate at least one language, Spanish, with the program in Grades 9–12. To assure continuity of learning, a single series of texts and related instructional materials was adopted. Every teacher uses, according to the level of learning and the learning capacities of the pupils, the following materials: student texts, laboratory tape sets (locally duplicated with permission of publisher), practice record sets, visual aids, a teacher's manual, and supplementary tapes and records for cultural instruction. In addition, each foreign language instructor has a tape recorder and a record player.

Although the materials selected and adopted were prepared for Grades 7–9 or 10–12, they could be used with little modification at the sixth-grade level. Experience of a year in the program has shown the procedure to be quite successful. Since it was recommended that pupils in the first part of Level I use no written materials, this phase of learning is purely audio-lingual.

No special tests are being used for placement or advancement. There is, however, need for formalized instruments of evaluation other than informal teacher evaluation of the students' abilities to understand, speak, read and write the foreign language. It is certain that adequate techniques and instruments for evaluation of student competency will be available soon either through the district's initiative and work, commercially, or both.

A Union High School District and Many Elementary Districts

Another outstanding example of developing a continuum of learning in the foreign language program was reported by a large high school district of seven four-year high schools. This district is served by many elementary school districts. The coordination and articulation of language programs is worked out with the assistance and collaboration of the foreign language coordinator on the county schools staff. The articulated foreign language program is described here from the response to a series of questions posed by the writer of this article.

The articulated foreign language program was planned by a foreign language subgroup of an organization known as the Heartland

Articulation Committee, which is composed of the assistant superintendents of nine elementary school districts and the Grossmont, Calif., Union High School District into which the elementary districts feed.

Planning and setting up the program was carried out by a Foreign Language Committee composed of representatives from all school districts in the Grossmont Union High School District area, with the county curriculum coordinator for foreign language serving as chairman. These representatives were, in most instances, foreign language teachers. Four days of consultant services were contracted for under NDEA Title III B in the area of articulation.

The planning work was carried out on a released time basis. Meetings were held at least once a month from 2 p.m. to 5 p.m. Substitute teachers were usually hired to teach each representative's class.

The Grossmont Union High School District, after three years of experiments with various kinds of materials for foreign language instruction, selected an audio-lingual text. Since all the school districts feeding into the high school district are presently teaching Spanish in the grades, and because members of the Articulation Committee were closely involved with the high school district in the matter of selection, the elementary school districts agreed to adopt the same materials in Grades 7 and 8 so that continuity of instruction could be more readily assured. It was further decided that Level I Spanish would be accomplished in the two years at the junior high school level (Grades 7 and 8). A series of sixteen two-hour teacher workshops in the use of the materials was established.

Special tests for achievement and placement have not been devised. However, a committee of elementary and high school teachers who will be employed during the summer will develop a list of terminal behavior goals for use in placement and measuring achievement. The final decision for placement in the high schools will be left to the junior high school teachers. The high schools will furnish to each junior high school a record of the success of the youngsters who are placed.

Teacher recommendations are written and sent on to the succeeding teacher, and, whenever possible, personal contacts are made between the teachers.

At the present time, Spanish is the only language taught in the elementary schools and continued into high school. It is hoped that other languages will be introduced in the elementary school districts in the future.

Some elementary school districts begin foreign language instruction in kindergarten while others begin in Grade 6 or 7. In any case, continuity is provided through the twelfth grade.

When a student enters high school, the "feeder" school should advise whether he belongs in Level I, II, III, or IV. The high school is prepared to accept the progress report of the junior high or elementary school, and this is as it should be. Nevertheless, not all the problems of foreign language articulation are completely solved in this area. A subcommittee of the Foreign Language Committee of the Heartland Articulation Committee is continuing to study the following problems: scheduling of foreign language in Grades 6, 7, and 8; sixth-grade course of study, materials, and equipment; and, evaluation and placement of pupils.

More Ideas and Suggestions for Articulation

The following ideas and suggestions for establishing and maintaining a continuum of learning in foreign language programs are proposed by the county and district education personnel.

1. Administrators and school boards should demonstrate enthusiasm for the program by providing every opportunity for teachers to improve teaching competence, e.g., by providing release time, by providing worthwhile workshops and materials of instruction, and by other means.

2. Elementary and secondary school teachers must accept one another professionally and must manifest mutual respect.

3. Teachers of the various levels of foreign language instruction must work together and share information.

(In our articulation program, the curriculum representatives from each of the districts meet and, among other things, discuss the problems of foreign language articulation. We then meet with the foreign language coordinators and the teachers. For example, the high school French teachers discuss articulation problems with the elementary school French teachers at meetings to which curriculum representatives and principals are invited. The basic problem is: What should a student be expected to know when he enters a second-year language class?)

4. The high school foreign language department should be involved in the development of the planning of the entire program.

(We were concerned that the high school teachers might have a traditionalist attitude toward foreign language instruction; however, this concern proved to be premature. The high school teachers have given inspiration to the program and should receive a large amount of credit for its success.)

5. The development of materials, courses of study, program adaptations, and counseling should be planned well in advance of putting the program into action.

(We feel we are well prepared now to move foreign language instruction down grade by grade to develop a truly sequential program. Although we have a smattering of Spanish teaching in our K-6 schools, it is fairly disorganized; thus far, we have concentrated on organization in Grades 7–12.)

6. A district should continue to use the services of outside-the-district paid language specialists. When finances permit, a district-level coordinator of the entire foreign language program for the district should be employed.

CHAPTER XII

Prospects for FLES

ROGER A. PILLET
University of Chicago

MANY consider Foreign Languages in the Elementary School one of the important recent innovations in foreign language teaching. It is natural that FLES, like any venture seeking a place among the vested interests, should have come under severe scrutiny, should have been supported by some and viewed with circumspection by others.

Currently, there is evidence that the future of FLES is not altogether secure. Fewer testimonials are reaching the journals. Rumours fly that programs are being abandoned. Allegedly, increasing enrollment in FLES classes is viewed with reservations as to the quality and continuity of the instruction taking place. Broad surveys voice a note of disappointment in the implementation of FLES programs.[1] By inference, "official" pronouncements suggest that perverse influences are operating to undermine many programs.[2]

My own reactions tend to be more optimistic. They may, however, reflect a prejudice in favor of FLES which, we hope, is based as much on experience with the movement as on formal and informal reporting. We have previously recorded these experiences[3] and hope that our report accurately communicated our convictions: FLES, in principle, is sound; a number of attending problems constitute a challenge to the profession; most of these problems can be minimized through enlightened effort.

Our work in FLES has continued and four years of observations subsequent to those reflected in our last formal report serve to confirm our original conclusions.* The information collected during this period still leaves us convinced that FLES is a worthy educational enterprise. We have a number of students who, on the basis of pronounciation and fluency, are living testimonials to the effectiveness of FLES. The long exposure provided by FLES has also resulted in gratifying results in the other, traditional, skills.†

We are dismayed that the proportion of students having reaped maximum benefit from the long exposure is indeed too small. Our efforts to find diagnostic measures, isolate factors relevant to motivation, structure sequences and devise materials more appropriate to individual aptitudes have, to date, shed light only on the complexity of the problem and on the limitations of our resources.

However, we are comforted by overall signs of gradual progress within our own program: better pacing of materials has resulted in fewer "casualties"; a more experienced staff, more careful structuring of the sequence are producing each year a better crop of FLES graduates (our sixth-graders now achieve roughly at the level of our former seventh-graders); our constant revision of the high school offerings is gradually minimizing the time and effort wasted in transition. We are confident that subsequent FLES classes completing a fourth year of French in the high school will be superior to our pilot groups.

Consonance between our own efforts and the experiences of others gives us reason to extend our optimism to the national scene. The fact that FLES has survived to date in spite of external pressures and internal problems attests to its present vitality and to the soundness of the premises upon which it was initiated. Temporary

* A final review of the achievement of our third- and fourth-grade starters (1955) is in process.

† Our successful fourth-grade starters are taking third-year college French courses (composition, literature) in their freshman college year: this had been one of our primary goals. Our better students among our third-grade starters achieve above the 75th percentile for eight semesters on the Cooperative French Test (Educational Testing Service) in or before the eleventh grade. Since these measures reflect only in part the total achievement of these students we are gratified that, for some at least, FLES has been a fruitful experience.

setbacks and sober re-appraisals may, in effect, be salutary, as they provide a more stable base for subsequent constructive efforts. A realistic analysis of limitations, assets, and potentials may indeed be prerequisite for judicious decisions and vigorous action.

The public (represented particularly by the parent group) is presently more understanding as to why Johnny, after relatively few hours of exposure to French, is not quite ready to drop English as his normal mode of communication. The school administrator (intent on maintaining balance in the curriculum) is less disturbed by the fact that he cannot reasonably justify the elimination of foreign languages from the secondary curriculum on the basis that entering FLES students are already "bilingual".

The teacher is less depressed as he observes that, notwithstanding generalizations about the universal capacity to learn a language, particularly demonstrable in the child, the range of achievement is as broad in foreign language as in other subjects.[4] He is more sensitive to degrees and kinds of motivation, more conscious of the ephemeral nature of initial enthusiasm. He is less reliant on the magic of culture as a deterrent to discouragement,* more willing to risk contamination lest the mystique of purity result in mystification.† He is less apologetic for eclecticism, having found it pedagogically sound though "scientifically" unsupported.‡

* It is not our intention to question the value of exposing the child to a foreign culture through foreign language study. We are suggesting that, for a number of students, the "cultural island" and a feeling of empathy for another people generated through the language process do not automatically neutralize a tendency to dejection and apathy resulting from a confirmed inability to achieve.

† We are referring to categorical dicta concerning total elimination of English in the classroom, normal speed of delivery, use of unrestricted vocabulary and structures, total avoidance of graphic materials for an indefinite period of time which, when applied beyond the point of common sense, leave a number of children in a state of perpetual perplexity and reduce the effectiveness of student–teacher rapport so essential in the early and middle grades.

‡ In spite of the fact that many of the linguistic principles on which current methods and materials are predicated are unquestionably sound, exclusive use of any single technique, format or medium must eventually reach a point of diminishing return in a normal classroom situation.

The post-honeymoon FLES teacher, alerted to practical difficulties of implementation and willing to exploit the available reservoir of experience, is in a far better position to translate theoretical injunctions into effective learning situations than was his precursor ten years ago.

There is available to him an extensive (perhaps too extensive) literature addressed to rationale, aims, methodology and practical suggestions.[5] A number of integrated courses and a plethora of guides and syllabuses leave him with an embarrassment of riches in making a choice;[6] advances in electronics and utilization of visual media properly geared to the demands of language teaching promise to alleviate increasingly and effectively one of the major stumbling blocks to FLES: the shortage of qualified teachers.* Increasing opportunities for in-service training supported at the local, state and national levels provide for a general though gradual improvement of the teaching corps and enhance the possibility of ever increasing effectiveness for FLES programs.

We anticipate that, in the next decade, work in a realistic climate, utilizing all available resources, selecting, systematizing, innovating, will surely secure the place of foreign languages in the elementary curriculum. We are nevertheless apprehensive that these prospects may be threatened by factors essentially external to FLES. Quality instruction in the grades is of no avail if not recognized as such and continued wisely in the secondary school. The transition, generally referred to as articulation, is one of the issues most vital to the future of foreign languages in the schools.†

---

* Slack, Ann, *et al.* (1960) *Parlons Français,* Heath–de Rochemont, Boston. Perhaps the most ambitious and well executed attempt to place a core of instructional and teacher-training audio-visual materials at the disposition of the nonspecialist teaching French in the grades. Pillet, R., and Garrabant, F., French with slides and tapes, *Elementary School Journal,* **62,** May 1962. A report of our own exploration of this teaching approach, using appropriate audio-visual materials of infinitely lesser scope.

† We are particularly concerned with extensive FLES problems (starting at third or fourth grade) as presenting more serious quandaries than the junior high school program, which can be considered merely an extension "downward" of the high school curriculum.

Articulation

Articulation has long been recognized as a difficult problem.*
It is perplexing that few allusions to the pains of transition appear in recent issues of foreign language journals, that procedures indicating how successful articulation has been achieved have not been described. The paucity of reports may be simply an index of waning interest in FLES. It may, on the other hand, lead to the supposition that articulation has been coped with satisfactorily.

Distressing are the rumors that, in some quarters, articulation has, indeed, caused no problem: all FLES students entering high school are simply enrolled in a beginning language class. There are unfortunate cases where, because of a modicum of achievement in any language skill due to insufficient contact hours or ill-devised instruction, grouping FLES students with those being exposed to the target language for the first time is justifiable. More often, however, the procedure is callously applied to children who demonstrate measurable achievement in the foreign language: the administrative officer, unrestrained (sometimes supported) by the chairman of the foreign language department, finds it uneconomical or inexpedient to modify the existing sequence. Even more shocking is the situation in which, although no fiscal or organizational limitations are evident, no provision is made for students with FLES experience because of an assumption that FLES is faddish, ineffective, that its aims are inconsistent with "good, solid" teaching, and that, if studiously ignored, it will surely pass away.

* Ericksson, Marguerite, Forest, Ilse, and Mulhauser, Ruth (1964) *Foreign Languages in the Elementary School,* Prentice-Hall, Englewood Cliffs, N.J. Articulation is described as "the extremely delicate and crucial point of the successful program" (p. 104). Reference (4) elaborates on valuable suggestions pertinent to articulation. The following quotation from a midwest curriculum director's letter points to a serious concern for the effect of articulation on the future of FLES: "I appreciate the suggestions you made though perhaps the greatest benefit is the assurance that you as well as other contacts I have made over the country are having similar problems with us in this curriculum area. I surely hope that someone is able to solve the difficulty which seems to be universal or I fear the practice of elementary French instruction will suffer sudden and violent demise in a great many school districts of the country."

We must assume that the most deplorable conditions are the result of incomprehension rather than ill will. Perhaps the magnitude of the task necessary to insure maximum articulation has been (and may still be) underestimated. We may all have skirted our responsibilities by relaxing our efforts short of the desired goals. Provisions for continuity do not automatically produce smooth articulation, long-range planning in no way insures proper implementation, carefully designed organizational machinery may have little influence on teacher morale and attitude.

Articulation is subject to the interaction of complex variables: the orientation and temperament of the elementary school staff in contrast with the high school staff; the degree of responsiveness of children to foreign language exposure (whether influenced by IQ, general academic orientation, locale, socio-economic background, etc.); the quality (goals, intensity of training, effectiveness of staff) and quantity (number of contact hours per week, total length of exposure) of the FLES program; the complexity of the organizational structure (number of students involved from one or several elementary schools within or outside the jurisdiction of a single administration). Channels of communication must be open in the conviction that there are certain goals, techniques, interests which are common to all foreign language teachers, that these areas of commonality are more relevant to essential issues than the overpublicized differences tending to obscure them. We submit that, within the continuum of foreign language teaching, such areas of commonality can provide a solid foundation for organized effort on the part of teachers at all levels.

Fractionating the Language skills

The burden of complaint among foreign language teachers has long been that too little time was available for the study of foreign languages and that, consequently, achievement in all language skills was not possible; hence, the fractionating of global objectives into "reading", "grammar", "conversation", each pursued to the detriment of the others.

FLES is intended to permit terminal achievement in *all* language skills to a greater degree because of the longer span of total exposure provided. Since FLES makes achievement of a common goal more feasible, comparisons restricted to the type of language activities better suited to more mature students are invidious indeed. FLES, in effect, reduces radically the basis for differences of opinion between exponents of the "traditional" method and teachers dedicated to the "New Key" or fundamental skill method as to the appropriate sequence for attacking the respective skills. Certain controversial aspects of the audio-lingual approach which are a matter of discretion (hopefully backed by some measure of rationality) at the high school level are imposed by the developmental stage of the learner in the grades. The child in third or fourth grade is certainly better equipped to develop understanding and to repeat accurately than he is to wrestle with the problems of "traditional" grammar. Deferring initiation to reading and writing until fifth or sixth grades is not only consistent with the sequence of attack suggested by the "New Key" but also timed appropriately with the consolidation of these skills in the child's native idiom. At the seventh- and eighth-grade level the student becomes mature enough to be encouraged to intellectualize about his previous exposure to the foreign language; he is capable of making generalizations of an increasingly sophisticated nature; analogizing can be systematically developed to relieve at least some of the burden imposed by rote learning.

The achievement of the student, successful during his extended experience in the grades, should be concrete and measurable but it need not be identical with the expectations of the secondary school. The FLES experience should be measured in terms of the number of language skills (or their components) contributing to the terminal goal rather than in terms of specific tasks considered terminal outside the total context of language learning.* The focal point of com-

* We are convinced that under relatively identical conditions (methods and materials) achievement at the elementary and the high school level is comparable. In our own program we have attempted to reduce the pangs of articulation by moving our elementary school program into the high school, equating first year French with third, fourth and fifth grades and second

monality, regardless of the sequence of presentation, is the *academic* nature of the experience: the elementary staff must be committed to a program which, though sometimes necessarily playful in nature, does not degenerate into a mere playful experience with foreign language overtones. The high school staff must be prepared to classify as academic achievement the degree of proficiency in the specific skills attacked, rather than the type and quantity of materials covered. It must build on what has been done, rather than lament the lacunae, which, in fact, provide the direction for continuing instruction.

Achievement inevitably reflects the corpus of materials to which students are exposed. Experienced teachers realize the complexities involved in changing from one type of text to another even when both are intended for the same level of instruction and the same age level. What then are the possibilities, present and potential, of structuring materials which, though prepared specifically for FLES, are appropriate as a foundation for high school instruction? Can the content of FLES and high school programs be summarized (and perhaps standardized) in such a way that, on the basis of commonality, a high school staff may anticipate and serve the needs of students entering from the elementary school? Ideally, what amount and what kinds of materials are coincident regardless of the age level for which instruction is intended?

We assume that selectivity must operate to some extent in the teaching situation. Since saturation of the student in the total language spectrum is not possible in the artificial situation of the

---

year French with sixth and seventh grades. Our better FLES students place out of this program and continue in special sections. Mediocre students and those exposed to less than five years in the grades are placed at appropriate points in the sequence. Students entering our school with no previous experience in French start at the beginning of the sequence, which, as we have indicated, is practically identical at both levels. Our observations (which we plan to formalize as we collect additional data) indicate our equation to be basically correct: in roughly the same number of contact hours (allowing for some "study" time expected of our high school population), the freshman group covers approximately the same materials with the same degree of proficiency (except for inferior pronunciation) as groups completing the fifth grade.

classroom, some decision is incumbent on the teacher as to what are initial, minimal goals, in contrast to unrestricted, long-range objectives. Materials appropriate to initiation and to each intermittent step, presented sequentially, should reflect patient organization rather than random choice.

We see the process of selection predicated on three separate though interrelated considerations: structure, vocabulary, and topical interest.

Structures, reputedly limited in number, hold the greatest promise for reasonably quick control.[7] Since, obviously, even a limited number of structures cannot be drilled simultaneously, it might prove useful to direct concerted effort and to reach a concensus as to a practical order in the sequence of presentation. The "grammaire" sections of *Français fondamental* 1e *degré* and 2e *degré* are already available to suggest priority at two separate levels.[8] Refinement of this research, a more precise breakdown of these two broad categories, based on classroom needs and experiences, would, it is to be hoped, provide a fundamental approach to structural content, facilitating evaluation of FLES performance and permitting subsequent instruction to begin at the precisely appropriate point. Surely, such a task is within the province and capacity of foreign language teachers.

The fact that vocabulary accretion is inherently a task of great magnitude makes it imperative to exercise restrictive (even arbitrary) measures in order to insure some common ground as to what lexical items should be available for the structure slots at various levels of instruction.

Again the "Centre d'étude du français élémentaire" has pointed the way. Our own attempt to elaborate on the word lists of *Français fondamental* 1e *degré* and 2^c *degré* have resulted in encouraging results: a basic list of some 1000 words common to adults and children and particularly appropriate to prereading instruction has emerged; an additional 1500 words can be roughly classified as to appropriateness to age level and to the language skill being attacked.*

* These word lists were scheduled for publication in the *French Review* in 1964–65.

Again, concensus on further subdivisions of this total word stock, sufficient for the entire FLES experience or for two years of high school instruction, would minimize the effect of vocabulary variations as a barrier to articulation.

A common approach to structure and vocabulary being within the realm of possibility, what are the prospects of arriving at common topics or situations which, without doing violence to lexical and structural restrictions, might be appropriate to the various age groups? A serious attempt has been made in the past to orient materials in such a way that they focus on "subjects" typically associated with specific age groups (animals in the early grades; social functions in the high school).

The specificity of these materials inevitably limits interchangeability. Furthermore, trying to keep pace with children's changing interests poses a problem particularly serious during the period of accelerated maturation encompassed by the span of the foreign language experience in question. The child, within the limits of the artificial learning situation, starting at zero linguistically, cannot hope to develop his language skills at a rate sufficient to cope with his desire to understand or express increasingly sophisticated ideas.

A systematic inquiry into what activities and situations possess a universal quality which cuts across age-level demarcations and therefore promises to be palatable to all students in the early phases of instruction might result in guidelines for materials appropriate to both the grades and the secondary school.

Though there is already agreement that certain topics are inevitable in the classroom situation (expressions of politeness, directions, etc.), others have infiltrated textbooks and syllabuses as a result of assumption and tradition rather than observation and analysis (e.g., telling time, the trip to the museum, etc.).

We suggest that interest in a specific group of situations might be sustained by shifting emphasis from topical to stylistic concerns. Students, regardless of their maturity, generally respond intuitively or rationally to beauty, humor, whimsy, these being perhaps more fundamental and generally stimulating than content. Cultural materials may be no exception to this generalization.[9]

Evaluation

Common measures of achievement are essential if FLES instruction is to be judged on its own merit and if continuing programs are to provide suitable instruction for incoming students.

Accepted current testing techniques using a predetermined, common, sequential schema of the structures and vocabulary appropriate at different levels of instruction as a frame of reference would insure accurate assessment of achievement and provide an essential diagnostic tool for those responsible for continuing instruction. The same framework would also permit evaluating *separately* the degree of competency in the components of respective language skills. Qualitative and quantitative measures applied appropriately to these components would reflect more accurately the total achievement of FLES students.

It seems justifiable to expect, for instance, that using the criterion of quality, pronunciation will be completely mastered in the course of FLES exposure, and that, similarly, oral reading will be taught to the point of near perfection in the grades. Other components such as aural comprehension, reading comprehension, fluency (spontaneity and accuracy), and writing (structural and spelling accuracy) need to be treated on a more quantitative basis which reflects the amount of material assimilated as well as the degree to which the basic processes have been mastered. Ideally, an incremental design for structures and vocabulary would permit analysis of the level of student performance in each component of the language skills. The same test items, administered in different ways would, for instance, reveal that student A comprehends the spoken word at the y level while being fluent only at the r level; he may be writing only at the b level due to the fact that his control of spelling (a level) is not commensurate with his control of structures (d level).

It should be noted that, under the system suggested, deficiencies are noted only with reference to the skill to which they are applicable. Proficiency is validated regardless of the level of instruction at which it was achieved. The tendency to deprecate FLES progress on the basis of inappropriate global evaluation is minimized. The student entering high school, his strength and weaknesses having been properly diagnosed, will continue in a coherent program which permits him to proceed from the specific points he had reached in the grades.*

Organization for a Continuous Foreign Language Program

The preceding paragraphs in essence constitute a plea for joint effort predicated on better communication. To translate common aims and practices into a functional program necessitates the kind of implementation which can best be achieved through sound organizational procedures. The scope of the organizational pattern should be as broad as possible; ideally, it should exist prior to the initiation of a program.

Without implying that the language teacher must abrogate his autonomy in the area of his particular expertise, we consider it unfortunate that administrators (regardless of their possible lack of competence in the foreign language) have not volunteered or have not been invited to play a sufficiently important role in solving the problem of articulation. It seems advisable to us that where there is disagreement as to methods and materials within and between staffs, the role of arbiter is best played by the administrative officer responsible for the total educational effort within the community. His is the responsibility to advise and administer in such a way as

* Unfortunately, we have at this time no constructive suggestion for dealing with the small number of students who, in spite of extensive exposure, demonstrate minimal command of any language skill. Our own experience with students in this category has been less than successful. The students identified as "unresponding" to the foreign language in the first two years of instruction have rarely made a miraculous recovery. None of the procedures tried has been a panacea: dropping from the course, ability grouping, special remedial work, transferring to another language on entering high school, have served only to point up the complexities attending the "nonlearner". The fact that such a student often has problems in other academic areas is but little consolation. It is indeed a grim prospect for the high school staff (heretofore committed only to "pulling through" poor students as they became identified) to devise effective strategies for students, often hostile to foreign language instruction, classified as nonperformers *before* they enter the secondary school class.

to protect the interest of the total program even though such procedures may, at times, infringe on preferences and convictions cherished by individuals on the respective foreign language staff. Furthermore, it is incumbent on the enlightened administrator to provide financial support and organizational opportunities for broader communication between staff at different levels of instruction in an effort to anticipate problems and mitigate differences through rational, discursive procedures.

Organization, regardless of its scope, cannot hope to operate effectively where too long deferred. Too often, no real concern for articulation is evident until a crop of FLES students is virtually sitting on the high school steps. The panic usually attending such a situation is inevitable. At this late date, judicious planning is most difficult, reactions to the *fait accompli* are characterized by resentment and resistance, some form of extemporization is seldom fruitful and the future looks glum indeed. The ultimate fate of a sound FLES program hinges to a great extent on the type of organization structured during the planning stages of the program. Realistically, if organizational problems, be they economic, administrative or personal, seem insurmountable at this early date, the prospect might best be given up or at least deferred until circumstances are more propitious.

Our remarks will be received with explainable diffidence: the foreign language teacher, perhaps as much as any other teacher, is apprehensive of encroachment and guards his autonomy jealously. However, the suggested elaboration of organizational patterns in which the administrative officer plays a major role is, in effect, a threat only to the type of parochialism which is difficult to condone. From the constructive point of view, organization opens channels of communication, permits exchange of points of view, leads, one may hope, to the mitigating of differences, and tends to redirect the total effort toward the child's learning experience as the central concern of instruction. The latter is surely a minimal point of commonality underlying our professional standards.

At the technical level, our suggestions for developing gradually and within the limits of possibility an outline reflecting concensus as to the sequence in which structures and vocabulary are to be taught and according to which they are to be measured by common instruments need not be construed as a move in the direction of regimentation. The teacher, secure as to *what* he is teaching, may approach his task with greater confidence and become more creative as to *how* he is teaching. A shift of emphasis to uniformity of content may, in fact, prove a salutary relief from conformity imposed by methodological tenets.

We reflect soberly on the magnitude of the effort required at the regional and national level to implement even partially the propositions submitted above. We are confident that our colleagues are capable of working out the minute practical details to a high degree of perfection.

We are concerned that failure to grapple seriously with the problem of articulation (in terms of ours or other suggestions) will have serious consequences. It is understandable that the secondary school teacher, under pressure to serve a rapidly increasing number of foreign language students, may be sorely tempted to dismiss FLES as a complicated, aggravating, additional burden. But this would be a disservice to the movement of FLES, sufficiently handicapped by a history of unsupported claims, improper implementation, disparate results, and would engender repercussions along the total continuum of foreign language teaching. Articulation between the elementary and secondary schools cannot, in principle, be disassociated from articulation between high school and college. Seriousness of purpose in attacking problems at one level must serve as a model for emulation at other levels. Mutual respect for the aspirations, achievements—and disenchantments—evident at respective stages of instruction is the only salutary antidote to the potential antagonism that, if allowed to undermine FLES, may threaten the total upper structure.

References

1. ALKONIS, NANCY V. and BROPHY, MARY A. (1961) A survey of FLES practices, *Reports of Surveys and Studies in the Teaching of Foreign Languages,* Modern Language Assoc., New York, pp. 213–17.

2. "A second statement of policy", developed and authorized by the Advisory and Liaison Committees of the Modern Language Association, *Modern Language J.*, **45,** 275 (Oct. 1961), speaks of the "dangers of inadequate attempts" to meet the need of an early start to foreign language learning.

3. DUNKEL, HAROLD B. and PILLET, ROGER A. (1962) *French in the Elementary School: Five Years' Experience,* Univ. of Chicago Press, Chicago.

4. *The Correlation of a Long Language Sequence Beginning in the Elementary School,* a report by the FLES Committee, American Assoc. of Teachers of French, mimeographed, 1963. Alludes to the problem of individual differences (p. 7).

5. PILLET, ROGER A. (Apr. 1959) Selected, annotated bibliography, *Elementary School J.* Annually since.
   NOSTRAND, HOWARD LEE (1962) *Research on Language Teaching: An Annotated International Bibliography for* 1945–61, Univ. of Washington Press, Seattle. Useful for references on research at the elementary school level.

6. *MLA Selective List of Materials* (1962) Modern Language Assoc., New York. A number of integrated courses of various scope and quality are listed and evaluated.
   KEESEE, ELIZABETH (1963) *References on Foreign Languages in the Elementary School,* U.S. Dept. of Health, Education and Welfare, OE 27008B, Washington, D.C. A list specifically prepared for the primary grades.

7. *Language Structure at FLES Level,* a report by the FLES Committee, American Assoc. of Teachers of French, mimeographed, 1962. Insists on the significance of structures in FLES teaching. We are merely suggesting the further development of this basic idea, with the objective of specifying what structures may best be taught during each phase of instruction.

8. *Le Français fondamental, premier degré. Le Français fondamental, deuxième degré* (1959), Chilton Company, Philadelphia.

9. ASPEL, PAULINE (Apr. 1963) Textes pour FLES, *French Review,* **36.**
   LAREW, LEONORA (Dec. 1960) Teach poetry to your primary students this way, *Hispania,* **43.**
   STEISEL, MARIE GEORGETTE (Mar. 1964) French poetry for children: a selected, annotated bibliography, *Modern Language J.,* **48.**

About the Contributors

P. Delattre

Pierre Delattre is a Professor of French and Phonetics and Director of the Research Laboratory of Experimental Phonetics at the University of California at Santa Barbara. He is best known for his work on the acoustics of speech by electronic synthesis and for some early experiments in language teaching techniques. He is now applying the manipulation of synthetic speech technique to the comparison of phonetic features in English, German, Spanish and French, with the objective of improving the teaching of foreign languages.

J. B. Carroll

John B. Carroll was born in 1916; he received a B.S. degree in classical languages at Wesleyan University and a Ph.D. in psychology at the University of Minnesota. He is a specialist in the psychology of language and is the principal author of the *Modern Language Aptitude Test*, widely used in selecting and placing students for foreign language study. He is Professor of Educational Psychology at Harvard University, and the author of *The Study of Language* (1953) and *Language and Thought* (1964). His professional memberships include the American Psychological Association, the Modern Language Association, the Linguistic Society of America, and the American Educational Research Association.

G. Newmark

Mr. Newmark has been a Human Factors Scientist with the System Development Corporation in Santa Monica, California, since 1955. As a member of the Education and Training Activity he has been conducting research in foreign language instruction and in programmed learning and participating in the design and operation of an experimental computerized educational laboratory.

He has engaged in extensive study in other countries and has taught foreign languages at all educational levels. He is a member of the California State Department of Education Foreign Language Advisory Committee and is presently Co-director of a California State Department research project on three different approaches to the teaching of Spanish in elementary schools.

A. Valdman

Albert Valdman, born in 1931, received his early schooling in France and received degrees from the University of Pennsylvania and Cornell University. He has taught at the Foreign Service Institute and Pennsylvania State

University, and is presently Chairman of the Department of Linguistics at Indiana University. His publications include books and articles in the area of French Linguistics and the application of linguistics to problems of second language learning.

G. A. C. Scherer

George A. C. Scherer has been Professor of Modern Languages at the University of Colorado since 1946. He began teaching in 1934. He holds a B.A. degree from the University of Illinois and an M.A. and Ph.D. degree from the University of Iowa. His chief interests are the training of language teachers and the improvement of foreign language teaching in schools and colleges. He has published numerous articles in professional journals, several texts and recently, with the psychologist Michael Wertheimer, *A Psycholinguistic Experiment in Foreign-Language Teaching* (McGraw-Hill, 1964).

G. Mathieu

G. Mathieu, Ph.D., Columbia University, has published in both the field of literature and pedagogy. Currently Professor of Foreign Languages at the California State College at Fullerton, he has also been Visiting Professor at five NDEA Summer Language Institutes and given addresses on modern language teaching here and abroad. He has published several texts, including a complete German audio-grammar. Active in many professional organizations, he is also the originator and publisher of *ML abstracts*, a quarterly of résumés relating to foreign language teaching. He believes that foreign languages are the keystone to a humanistic education.

P. Pimsleur

Paul Pimsleur was born in New York City on October 17, 1927. He received his bachelor's degree from City College of New York. He received the Ph.D. degree in French from Columbia University in 1956; he received a Master's degree in Psychology from Teachers' College, Columbia, in 1957. He was a member of the French Department at U.C.L.A. from 1957 until 1961; since 1961 he has been Director of the Listening Center and Associate Professor of Romance Languages at the Ohio State University. He is the author of a series of aptitude and proficiency tests in French, Spanish and German; he has prepared programmed courses in French, Spanish and Modern Greek; he has written numerous articles for professional journals.

J. M. Stein

Jack M. Stein is Professor of German and Chairman of the Department of Germanic Languages and Literatures at Harvard University. He is the author of *Richard Wagner and the Synthesis of the Arts*; three textbook anthologies, *The German Heritage* and *The German Scientific Heritage* (both with Reginald Phelps), and *Schnitzler–Kafka–Mann* (with Henry Hatfield); and numerous pedagogical and literary articles and reviews.

Mr. Stein is Advisory Editor for German texts for W. W. Norton & Co. and a member of the Advisory Committee for the Foreign Language Program of the Modern Language Association.

F. W. Nachtmann

Francis W. Nachtmann, Ph.D., Associate Professor of French, has served on the faculty of the University of Illinois since 1948. His doctoral thesis concerned the medieval French epic, but his academic career has been primarily directed toward improving teaching methods and teacher training. Besides devising a program for training college teaching assistants, he also originated a course on language laboratory techniques, and organized the reading French courses for doctoral candidates, for which he has produced a textbook: *French Review for Reading Improvement* (Macmillan 1965). He was director of the language laboratory from 1959 to 1965 and currently is coordinator of elementary and intermediate French courses.

D. M. Feldman

David M. Feldman is currently Professor of Applied and Descriptive Linguistics at California State College at Fullerton. He received his Ph.D. degree from Cornell University and has taught at Cornell, Princeton, and Colorado Universities. He has directed and established programs in general linguistics, taught in and directed NDEA language institutes, and has taught in the Peace Corps training program. He is a frequent speaker at professional meetings in the United States and abroad, is the author of books and articles in the fields of applied and theoretical linguistics, and has been the director of various government- and institution-sponsored research projects.

E. V. O'Rourke

Everett V. O'Rourke, M.A., is consultant in secondary education, California State Department of Education, with special responsibilities for instruction and curriculum in foreign languages and English. He has had many years experience as a teacher, supervisor and administrator in the school districts and counties in California as well as instructor in teacher education institutions. He has been a director and an active member of state and national committees, seminars and workshops for the improvement of instruction in languages. He has collaborated in the authorship of guides for the teaching of languages such as: *Spanish—Listening, Speaking, Reading, Writing; French—Listening, Speaking, Reading, Writing; Language Instruction—Perspective and Prospectus*.

R. A. Pillet

Although born in France, most of Mr. Pillet's formal education and professional experience took place in the United States. Subsequent to obtaining an A.B. and an M.A. from the University of Missouri he taught French at that university, at Washington University, and at Northwestern University, where he completed the Ph.D. degree in 1955.

Accepting a position at the University of Chicago at that date he became interested and involved in the establishment of a FLES program in the University of Chicago Laboratory Schools and has since that time devoted an increasing amount of his time and energies to the movement. Currently, as Associate Professor of Education in French, he is involved in the teacher training program of the Graduate School of Education and is Chairman of the Foreign Language Department of the Laboratory School.

Besides a number of articles, Mr. Pillet's contributions to FLES have ranged from the preparation of materials (*En Classe,* Coronet Films, 1961; *Mon Premier Dictionnaire,* World Publishing Co., 1962) to more basic research findings as illustrated by the book co-authored with Harold B. Dunkel, *French in the Elementary School: Five Years' Experience* (Univ. of Chicago Press, 1962).

DATE DUE

7/9			
JUL 26 1968			
MAR 1 1969			
SEP 29 1969			
OCT 21 1969			
MAR 3 1970			
MAR 9			
MAR 19 1971			
MAY 13			
NOV 22 1971			
MAR 14 1972			
GAYLORD			PRINTED IN U.S.A.